Networking Karma

Networking Karma: How Today's Cutting Edge Networking Trends Can Help You Connect and Conquer

For information about this title or to order other books and/or electronic media, contact the publisher:
Speednetworx™
http://www.consultnetworx.com/speednetworx/
info@networkingkarmabook.com

Library of Congress Control Number: 2015911902

ISBN: 978-0-9883834-0-1

Printed in the United States of America

Networking Karma

How Today's Cutting Edge Networking Trends Can Help You Connect and Conquer

Gail Tolstoi-Miller

Dedicated to my late father,
Mel Tolstoi

"Remembering that I'll be dead soon is the most important tool I've ever encountered to help me make the big choices in life. Because almost everything—all external expectations, all pride, all fear of embarrassment or failure—these things just fall away in the face of death, leaving only what is truly important. Remembering that you are going to die is the best way I know to avoid the trap of thinking you have something to lose. You are already naked. There is no reason not to follow your heart."

~ Steve Jobs

And to the most important men in my life:
my two sons, Mel and Holden.
Every day you teach me something new
and keep me on my toes. I will always
love both of you unconditionally.

"I find the great thing in this world is not so much where we stand, as in what direction we are moving; we must sail sometimes with the wind and sometimes against it...but we must sail, and not drift, nor lie at anchor."

~ Oliver Wendell Holmes, Sr.

ACKNOWLEDGEMENTS

ALTHOUGH I HAVE BEEN COACHING, speaking and writing on the subject of networking for several years, today I understand much, much more about the finer points of building relationships than when I first embarked upon the writing of this book.

Throughout the research and writing process, I applied the principles of *Networking Karma* initially to connect with (and then to benefit from) a variety of experts whom I now consider a part of my "guidance alliance"—friends and associates who so generously shared their help and expertise. I've said it before—and I'm saying it here again—I will always be available to help or support them in any endeavor. I can't thank these folks enough.

First and foremost, I have to thank my amazing husband, Bruce, who is always there with love and support for me in all of my endeavors.

Also, a special thanks goes to Erica Wasserman, who assisted me in every aspect of writing this book. Her attention to detail, excellent listening skills, and intuition helped to hone my stories and crystalize my messages. Erica's natural writing style perfectly captured, realigned and enhanced my thoughts and words.

Teresa Marinelli, my transformational guru. Thank you for arming me with the toolbox I used to reach this and other goals. Together, you and I have moved many obstacles. Thank you for helping me along on this journey—I'm so lucky to have had you as my guide!

My colleagues deserve a nod here, too. Many have trusted me with their business needs and I'm proud of each and every unique relationship I've developed through the years. I love what I do and I'm committed to giving everything I've got to ensure your success.

As for my staff—I say it all the time—great companies are driven by awesome people. Thank you for working with me to build a company with a culture as unique and energetic as each of you!

To my mom: From the bottom of my heart I thank you for always being there for me. I don't tell you enough but I appreciate you more than you know. The same goes for my brother, Robert, and sister, Elissa, both of whom I love unconditionally.

A special shout-out to Darren Prince of Prince Marketing Group.

Thank you to *Networking Karma's* amazing content contributors, who have given generously of their insight. Every person who scans these pages will be enriched professionally and personally, thanks to your collective wealth of knowledge. Complete contact information for each contributor is listed at the end of this book.

Many people, from editors to designers to publicists, were involved in bringing this book to life. I want to thank everyone who played a part in this project—there are too many to thank. You know who you are!

And finally, to all of those larger-than-life mavericks who inspire me: Richard Branson and the late Steve Jobs. Even Ozzy Osbourne! Thank you for proving that you can do things authentically and differently and still succeed...wildly!

PREFACE

FINDING A JOB. Building a business. Hiring employees. Learning trends. Attracting opportunities. Maintaining relationships. Getting referrals. Spreading word of mouth.

There are many reasons why you may need to network. But when you get to the core of why you MUST network, it is really quite simple.

Your infinite potential, the very best person that you can be, may very well lie in the hands of another person; someone you have yet to meet.

Does this statement sound daunting to you? Well, never fear. You see, life is one huge networking opportunity. We all network every day without even realizing it. And this book is brimming with stories, strategies and secret to-dos so you can network better.

Today, thanks to Speed Networking, it's easier and more fun than ever to cast a wide net and meet a variety of people who all want to meet you, too. And there are other tools at your disposal—social media, savvy self-marketing and good old-fashioned etiquette—that can help you shape those connections into meaningful, give and get relationships.

But a true, meaningful network of connections does not happen overnight. Building your network requires an ongoing commitment and total dedication to the process. It is not so much hard work as it is a labor of love. Phone calls, emails, social media posts, lunches, favors and introductions are only some of the many tasks that capable networkers perform on a daily basis.

Getting into the networking groove takes discipline, consistency and a true goal of giving. Even after the newness and excitement of networking wears off, your persistence must be fierce. Why? Because with every effort you put forth, you'll shore up the links in your chain of connections for mutual benefit and success.

In 2008, a study was conducted by researchers at the University of Erlangen-Nuremberg. The goal was to gain a better understanding of the relationship between networking and career success. The results revealed that "networking is not only related to concurrent salary and career satisfaction, but also to salary growth over time." While it is comforting to know that research has been done to support these assumptions, common sense tells us that if we surround ourselves with smart, connected and committed fellow networkers, our lives can be moved in all sorts of positive directions.

Hundreds of books have been written about networking and the nurturing that is required to sustain relationships. Seminars on the topic have been attended by tens of thousands. And of course, networking groups like Business Network International™ (BNI™) and Le Tip™ have built strong followings and golden reputations due to their winning business platforms. Eventually, every serious networker comes to the same conclusion—either through reading, learning or actually doing—that the development of contacts requires a very slow, very patient approach.

So Speed Networking (my preferred form of networking) might, at first glance, seem counterintuitive. After all, how can an event featuring dozens of fast-paced and sometimes quite arbitrary meetings between strangers help you in the slow and steady development of individual relationships?

Well, if all of my secrets were revealed here in the preface, there would be no need for you to read on. So you'll have to delve into these pages to discover how to get the most from Speed Networking and beyond! I'll also share my tried-and-true tips that you can use to enhance all of your relationship-building efforts. From first impressions to event follow-ups, I'll give you the advice you need to connect and conquer every networking situation.

As you explore these chapters, you'll be inspired by how others have effectively increased their personal networks through Speed Networking. You'll also discover how to implement different Speed Networking applications and how to foster your newfound relationships to further yourself and your contacts in every aspect of life.

When you get to CHAPTER 3 of this book, describing the format of Speed Networking events, you may find yourself saying, "I could never do that!" If you hear a negative voice in your head, push through the nerves and the self-doubt. After all, as a self-proclaimed introvert, I understand the uneasiness that accompanies the typical networking experience. But Speed Networking is not typical and it is geared toward those of us who aren't the type to "work a crowd."

Throughout this book you will see dozens of simple To-Dos, identified by the symbol shown at right: ☑ These To-Dos are tactics I have culled from experts and associates to help you boost your networking success—fun, simple exercises and ideas you can implement immediately.

Remember, everyone has what it takes to be a successful networker. All you need is a little preparation, practice and patience.

You have the power to transform your life through the relationships you develop. Do it and you'll find true joy and satisfaction from helping others too.

If I can do it, you can do it! Read on and find out how easy it is!

CONTENTS

INTRODUCTION

THIS BOOK IS TANGIBLE. You can hold it in your hand. Use it as a tool. Share it with your friends and business associates. You can put it on a shelf and refer to it at any time. It is paper and ink, filled with ideas to help and inspire you to further yourself in every part of your life.

However, the core of this book—the real, true meaning behind every word I've written here—is based on a simple and esoteric idea, one you cannot touch or feel: Karma.

What is Karma?

Webster's Dictionary defines the term Karma as, "the force generated by a person's actions held in Hinduism and Buddhism to perpetuate transmigration and in its ethical consequences to determine the nature of the person's next existence."

Put in layman's terms: "What goes around comes around." And that is ultimately what networking—in any form—is all about.

So throw away your preconceived notions. Networking is not *just* about growing your business, making your sales quotas or finding your next job. Networking is not *just* about YOU or YOUR goals. Networking is about Karma. It's about giving and then getting back what you give, at some later time. The most successful networkers look at each connection as an opportunity to do a good deed, to share knowledge and to offer assistance or guidance. In fact, the most successful networkers are on a constant mission of "giving."

And that is exactly why I am writing this book. By sharing my knowledge about Speed Networking and imparting my experiences, I will help you to reach your full potential, to be smarter and happier for the contacts you make, and to be enriched by the relationships you develop.

Part I
KARMA

Chapter 1
BELIEVE!

"Sometimes all you need is twenty seconds of insane courage and something great will come of it."
~ Benjamin Mee, We Bought a Zoo

So, you want to improve your life through networking! Perhaps you've considered focusing more of your efforts on networking but somehow your plans never got off the ground. You may be frustrated. You know networking is something you should be doing. But you make excuses.

You procrastinate.

You think of reasons why you'll start next month or after the holidays.

You build your New Year's resolutions around your goal to network better.

There always seems to be a time constraint or another priority that pushes your networking to the back burner….Why?

Are you lazy? Spineless? No doubt you've gotten down on yourself about this stagnation many times. But I'm guessing there's no mystery behind this. There's a reason you're stuck in this rut of inaction.

And it isn't weakness, laziness or any other negative trait you may think you have. You're stuck because deep, deep down inside, you may not believe you're capable of being a successful networker. **You are letting self-limiting beliefs get the best of you.**

In these next few pages I will explore the power of a positive belief system and how you can remove negative beliefs that are getting in your way. Everyone, INCLUDING YOU, is capable of choosing the beliefs that will propel you and your networking forward, and of squashing the beliefs that hold you back!

What Are Beliefs?

Very simply, beliefs are DEEPLY HELD feelings and ideas you have about yourself, your place in the world, your relationships and your abilities. Beliefs can be positive or negative. They can move you toward action or keep you stuck in a rut. Negative beliefs stem from the little critic living inside your head, who can be quite vocal at times, frequently finding fault and questioning your capabilities.

This little critic inside your head seems logical. He knows you well. And you've always trusted him to guide you. But here are some things you should know about the critic and the negative beliefs he feeds you.

Where Do Beliefs Originate?

Many of the beliefs in your head stem from your childhood. Cultural attitudes (about appearance, education, work ethic or social status) play a partial role in forming your personal belief system. Educators also affect the development of self-limiting beliefs. But more than anything or anyone, it is your parents and their own beliefs—about themselves and you—that shape your belief system.

As a child, no doubt you were exposed to comments and critiques, and you took them to be truths. Perhaps your current beliefs about networking are based on statements you heard as a child, such as:

- "She is so insecure!"
- "He got the looks but his sister got the brains."
- "She takes after me—she is so shy!"
- "He is such a scatter-brain!"
- "She has brains but no common sense...."

From Santa Claus to the Tooth Fairy, children are led to believe many things by the adults in their lives. But some of the beliefs are negative and can be dangerous to the psyche. As we grow, we tend to internalize and generalize what others believe and expect of us. These beliefs become our own personal truths and can hold us back from recognizing our full potential.

Many people who believe they can't be effective at networking are basing this belief on societal influences or things that adults said about them when they were just children!

Beliefs Are Not Truths So Why Do They Exist?

Here's a story about negative beliefs and my friend Alex.

Alex believes he does not have the skills to be a success at networking events. He will give you all sorts of reasons to support this belief. As a youngster, he was so shy that he was afraid to answer the telephone when it rang. In his teens, his parents always yelled at him to, "make eye contact," frequently and publicly embarrassing him about this. While in college, Alex was the only freshman guy in his dorm who was uncomfortable with the whole idea of pledging a fraternity, and never did.

Alex's belief—that he is an awful networker—is based on his personal laundry list of previous experiences. It is evident that one or more painful experiences can encourage life-altering, self-limiting beliefs and can become major components of our self-concept.

Significant and painful events carry more weight in our psyche than everyday life events. When it comes to networking, Alex has more negative examples than positive ones. It is easier for Alex to look for evidence that supports his negative belief about his networking ability. But holding on to these beliefs protects Alex from ever having to fail or look foolish, because he can choose to avoid networking entirely. In reality, he would certainly be able to network as well as anyone IF he wanted to do it very much and was willing to put in the time and effort required to do it well.

Alex's limiting beliefs are getting in the way of his ability to network.

And this is interfering with his professional success. But he is reluctant to let go of this negative belief. *Why?* Because his belief about his inability to network has served him well for years. *It has given him permission not to try.*

Your negative beliefs are no truer than your positive ones, so make a choice! Pick the beliefs that move you toward personal and professional successes, not away from them!

Changing Your Negative Beliefs

The first step in changing your negative beliefs is to acknowledge and own them. Doing so deflates your negative beliefs. Take Alex, for example. He believes that he does not have the skills to be a success at networking events. However, upon closer examination, Alex can find PLENTY of evidence to support the contrary. After all, he has a warm, welcoming smile; he has many wonderful and committed friends; and he has always succeeded in leadership positions, from student council in grade school to being a TA in college. These are valuable and necessary qualities for networking success. These qualities are not just beliefs; they are truths about Alex. And they are much more tangible than the beliefs he has been allowing to rule his behavior.

Marci Wolf Ober, LMFT, is a licensed family therapist who runs a private practice in northern New Jersey. She works with adults, adolescents and families to help them live optimally. In addition to speaking frequently on topics such as "Understanding Anxiety" and "Family Dynamics," she has graciously shared her vital list of To-Dos—powerful tips for "Conscious Creation" of an optimal "Internal Guidance System":

To-Dos

1. **OWN IT:** If you don't own it, you have no ability to change it. Change is not easy. But not changing is even harder! Awareness is the first key step.

2. **FOCUS ON THE RESULTS OF THE GOAL:** At first, do not focus on the "How," but imagine engaging successfully in the desired behavior, outcome or experience. For example, if the goal is to lose ten pounds, picture yourself ten pounds lighter. Imagine yourself feeling the lightness and confidence that comes from that. Place yourself there and feel the great feeling that

comes with the image. Stay with that image and connect with positive feelings for as long as possible.

3. **WATCH FOR ROAD BLOCKS:** At some point, obstacles will appear. They will encourage your inner critic to say things to you like, "You have tried this before, just forget it! It is just too hard." Pay attention to this as an observer, because that is the very self-limiting belief that you will want to own and rework! Remember: just because you have a self-limiting belief does not mean it is true! Understand that the belief itself needs be challenged and reworked. You must take control of your "belief critic." Evaluate the effectiveness potential of your core beliefs around the issue at hand.

4. **GO BACK TO THE GOAL:** Imagine the result of being successful. Discover the great feeling that comes to you when you connect emotionally with what you really want. At this point, you have an outline of the process. You can see what you want. You recognize what resistance is holding you back. Now the hard work of change can begin! Bring it on, Baby!

5. **REROUTE NEURAL PATHWAYS:** This can make an introvert more able to connect easily with others, a sales professional or athlete more successful, a parent more artful with her children. They all involve conscious cultivation of certain traits and a willingness to invest some time and effort (even a little) toward the goal. They include:

    - Visualization: Direct your focus on the desired outcome. There are many methods to visualization but most involve relaxation and mental imagery of the goal. The more senses involved, the stronger the process.

- Yoga is amazingly effective in cultivating the ability to detach from, and more neutrally observe the mind/body. This is very helpful in seeing (rather than being fused with) self-limiting beliefs. Yoga can also strengthen the ability to be more poised and open to what is possible regarding self-promoting possibilities!

- High-quality therapy or other supportive processes of self-inquiry. Come to understand the origins or roots of your personal belief system. This can be a huge time saver and incredibly helpful in achieving your goals. Remember, what we can own and work on is what we can change!

- Inspiration: Seek examples of those who live your goal. Expose yourself to people who do, have, or are what you want for yourself. Watch for and try to understand what their belief systems include and be open to trying them on. For example, a person who attends networking functions regularly probably has a belief system that supports rather than sabotages networking success.

6. **BELIEVE:** The strongest and most lasting change happens with the greatest intensity and frequency of thought and emotion. The greatest accomplishment is making it to the starting line. The game is won or lost before we actually play. Most of us talk ourselves out of our dreams before we ever embark on creating them.

A Study in Visualization

One of the most powerful "mind tools" is visualization. It has been credited with unlocking the physical, emotional and spiritual potential of millions of people in search of personal growth.

Visualization IS NOT pie in the sky psychobabble; there is proof that it works! Dozens of studies have revealed the benefits of visualization.

As far back as 1943, The Journal of General Psychology reported on the effects of mental practice in the acquisition of motor skills.

Part of this study evaluated the effects of visualization (or mental practice) on basketball players. The free throw percentage of a group of basketball players was being measured and assessed. To establish a baseline for the research, the initial free-throw success rate of each player was evaluated and recorded. The athletes were then divided into three random groups. After about three weeks of research, their free throw success rate was re-evaluated. The results were as follows:

- The first group, which physically practiced shooting free-throws for an hour daily, collectively improved their free-throw shooting by twenty-four percent.
- The second group, which practiced daily by visualizing (mentally practicing) the act of shooting successful free-throws, collectively improved their free-throw shooting by a shocking twenty-three percent without having physically shot a basketball during the previous three weeks!
- The third group, which neither physically practiced nor visualized shooting free-throws, showed no increase in percentage.

Just imagine how visualization might help you to improve your networking performance! Pick up a book or Google the concept for more information.

Chapter 2

READY, SET, SPEED NETWORK!

"It's not about what you've done,
It's about what you doing.
It's all about where you going
No matter where you've been. Let's go!"
~ Calvin Harris, Ne-Yo

OKAY, READER. Now that you've discovered the core of your self-limiting belief and re-routed your "Internal Guidance System," you are ready to explore networking and life, and how you can get the most out of both.

Throughout these pages, I'll act as your tour guide, showing you the many roads you can take on your journey to networking success.

Let's start with the road less traveled: Speed Networking. In the words of famed poet Robert Frost:

> "*. . . Two roads diverged in a wood, and I—*
> *I took the one less travelled by,*
> *and that has made all the difference.*"

Wondering why I'm quoting a legendary American poet in a book about networking? Well, on my road to success, my networking journey took me in many different directions. Like the inspiring walker of Frost's *The Road Not Taken,* when I decided to travel on the Speed Networking path, taking the road less travelled made ALL the difference in my personal and professional life.

As far as I know, there has never been a published work dedicated to exploring Speed Networking that provides as much detail as I will here. So buckle up, rev up your engine, put the pedal to the metal and let's go.

This Speed Networking trailblazer is ready to tell all!

What Is Speed Networking?

You've probably heard the term Speed Dating and assumed that Speed Networking is similar. Well, it is. And it isn't.

First, the similarities: like Speed Dating, Speed Networking follows the round-robin approach to connecting with others. In both cases, people gather in a large meeting area (maybe a restaurant, conference hall or catering facility) and have an opportunity for brief, informative exchanges, meeting with a dozen or more individuals during the course of a single event.

Now, the differences (and they are dramatic!).

The goal of Speed Dating is to connect with just one, perfectly suited individual. Participants quickly whittle down the group of potential suitors with the intent of honing in on the one, mutually attractive match.

Speed Networking, on the other hand, is all about improving the quality *and* quantity of your connections. The object is to meet and connect with as many Speed Networkers as possible. Unlike Speed Dating, attendees are not there to eliminate new contacts, they are there to cast a wide net and develop relationships with a variety of people. This formula works well for a number of reasons.

Why Speed Networking Works

The last time you went to a business mixer or conference, you probably met a guy like Larry. Larry knows the name of every cashier at his local market. The tellers at his bank greet him by his first name every time he goes in to make a deposit or withdrawal. When Larry takes his family out to dinner, he makes sure to connect on a personal level with all of the waitstaff. Larry can't even walk into an elevator without striking up a conversation with his fellow riders.

When it comes to business, Larry can walk into a room full of people and absolutely light up. He makes it his personal mission to say "hello" to everyone in attendance. His directness and confidence radiates from within and his charisma actually works like a magnet, drawing people toward him.

Needless to say, Larry loves to attend networking events.

And then there are the rest of us! Those of us who find networking events awkward and uncomfortable. And why shouldn't we? Making small talk with total strangers is painful. Conversations run out of stamina and bowing out of them gracefully is never easy. Sometimes, fellow networkers recognize the oncoming slow, stale rhetoric and make it easy to slink away. But others verbally lasso you, and then drag you down into the quick sand of useless chatter that becomes absolute torment to escape.

Thankfully, Speed Networking empowers attendees to completely sidestep these unbearable networking situations. The event's structure provides a brief platform for each person to speak, and then there is a clean breakaway point that requires you to move on to the next match-up. There is no time for yawning, rejection or running for the door!

Because Speed Networking has been proven to be more effective than traditional networking methods, Speed Networkers can develop more contacts in one evening than most business people do in five months. Whether you're an entrepreneur, student, business development professional or a group member of any kind, you'll appreciate this uniquely structured, targeted, low-pressure form of networking. The entire process is facilitated for ease and efficiency.

The organized time structure of Speed Networking also allows you to sharpen your networking skills by practicing and perfecting your "Elevator Pitch." You'll also enhance your confidence and be able to conquer less-structured social and business events (more on this later in the book). Ultimately, Speed Networking makes it possible for you to soak up information and ideas to help build your business and enhance your life. As an added benefit, Speed Networking helps to elevate your reputation as someone who is well-connected and "in the know."

Speed Networking is also FUN! The atmosphere at these events is not tense or stuffy, but exciting and adrenaline-fueled. The enthusiasm at a typical Speed Networking function becomes contagious and even the most reserved or uncomfortable networkers are buoyed by the tone, informality and shared goal of all attendees—that is, to meet and help each other!

My Speed Networking Story

Although I am a seemingly normal, self-adjusted and successful professional woman with a stable family life and a comfortable circle of friends, I have a personal quality that is, in some respects, both a strength and a weakness: I'm an introvert!

If you didn't know me—and if you watched me in action as a Speed Networking host—you would probably think just the opposite. However, the fact remains that, even at an early age, I displayed the signs of reticence. I averted eye contact, spoke very quietly and clung to the comfort of teachers or my parents. I never spoke to my classmates and was even bullied due to my extreme introverted nature. In fact, as a kindergartener I was so reserved and kept to myself so much that the educators at my elementary school asked my parents to consider holding me back to allow my socialization skills to "catch up" with the other kids. It took a long time for me to warm up to others and I spent a lot of time observing from the sidelines.

Today, many years later, fragments of my inner child remain. While I do enjoy the company of others, I am not a fan of large gatherings. I feel most comfortable in the company of my nearest and dearest.

No, I do not have a social anxiety disorder or agoraphobia; however as the CEO of a consulting business, I had to acknowledge—with dread—the need to network. The thought of actually entering a crowded room, being surrounded by strangers, having to begin conversations, find common ground and engage in meaningful, open-ended exchanges has always made me cringe, shudder and stress out. Still, I have endured many networking functions.

It's common knowledge that networkers gravitate toward attendees they already know, thus avoiding (sometimes successfully) the need to leave their comfort zones. In fact, the average number of new connections made at a networking event is two or three people. This low number underscores how limiting most networking experiences really are. Clearly, most networkers do not fully optimize their networking opportunities. I know this first hand because this would commonly happen to me when I attended networking functions.

One day, I saw an ad promoting a Speed Networking event and decided to give it a try. While attending my first Speed Networking event, I had my "aha moment." After experiencing the relief, ease and success of this event, I jumped in with both feet, started my own Speed Networking company, and never looked back.

A Brief History of Speed Networking

A relatively young concept, Speed Networking seems to have originated simultaneously here in the US, and abroad, in the UK. The event format is an off-shoot of the Speed Dating phenomenon which was started around 1999 by a rabbi in California as a means of connecting young Jewish singles in the Los Angeles area. The concept of Speed Dating took off in the United States, and before long there were hundreds of companies running these match-making events.

According to *BusinessWeek Magazine,* "Speed Networking was first utilized during the US economic downturn of the early 2000s and began rising in popularity as the decade drew to a close. Credit for applying Speed Dating concepts to the corporate world has been attributed to Tom Jaffee, a Columbia MBA alumnus and founder of a speed-dating network."

Chapter 3

HOW TO SPEED NETWORK

"Expose yourself to your deepest fear; after that, fear has no power, and the fear of freedom shrinks and vanishes. You are free."

~ Jim Morrison

The Big Picture

IMAGINE THIS. It's 7 p.m. You anxiously walk into a large meeting area (maybe a restaurant, conference hall or catering facility) and go straight to the check-in desk. You are greeted by smiling hosts. They introduce themselves and ask for your name. They sign you in and help you with your name tag. All around, there are men and women, young and not so young, all looking anxious but eager to make your acquaintance.

Can you guess what the most commonly asked question is during these pre-event mingles?

"Is this your first time Speed Networking?"

That's usually all it takes to get the wheels of conversation turning. Pairs quickly meld into groups and before long there are others joining in on the chatter. Perhaps there are pass-around snacks or a light meal to enjoy, and sometimes a complimentary cocktail or a cash bar are part of the event.

Regardless of these details, the event has officially begun.

Before long, the moderator welcomes everyone to the event, asks attendees to take a seat and introduces herself. She provides some tips on how to successfully Speed Network. Sometimes a guest speaker or even a comedian is invited to further inform and/or entertain the group.

The layout of the room and the sequence of events are discussed, questions are answered, and each person is seated in a predetermined starting spot. A bell or whistle (or some other loud prompter) is sounded to signal the start of the first round.

Introductions commence; the first brief exchange takes place. After a set period of time, attendees make an orderly move and the process begins again. Once everyone has met each other (or time has run out, whichever comes first) the evening ends with a less-structured time to mingle. Sometimes dessert and coffee are served, an opportunity for follow-up conversations is provided, and the evening draws to a close as the last stragglers are ushered out the door—generally too engrossed in conversation to realize that the event has ended and the staff and planners are tired and want to go home!

Break the Ice

Perhaps the biggest challenge for new Speed Networkers is finding a way to ease into the evening's events. Most networking event planners implement ice-breakers to facilitate introductions and energize participants. At my Speed Networking events, I provide a pen and name tag and ask participants to jot down an interesting and unexpected term to describe themselves, which could include anything from "Hole-in-one" to "Doodle Lover" to "Twin."

Corny? Contrived?

Maybe, but this small description is generally enough to fuel the conversation for the first awkward moments of the event. It helps to put people at ease.

One point I'd like to make here: a few name tag terms are "off limits" at my events, namely business titles and company names. Last year, one of my event attendees was the CFO of a mid-sized manufacturing firm. Without my knowledge, she wrote CFO on her nametag. Within ten minutes of the beginning of the early-evening mingling session, there were people lined up to make her acquaintance. It was obvious that the other attendees were motivated to connect with the CFO because of her purchasing power at her company.

Personally, I believe every Speed Networker—indeed, every networker—should avoid passing judgment on people because of their job title or social status. It is foolish and short-sighted to EVER disqualify someone from your network because of some preconceived notion you might have of them or their ability to "help" you achieve your goals. In networking, and in life, everyone should be on equal ground, approached for genuine interest and not just because of a lofty title.

Passing Judgment: Are You Guilty of This?

My husband is a chef/restaurateur. As you can imagine, his hours are long and our two busy careers make it difficult for us to share quality time. A few years ago, I decided to help out at the restaurant on Saturday nights. It gave my husband and me some additional time together and he liked having me there on the busiest night of the week to oversee operations.

Occasionally, I filled in as a waitress. One evening, I had to serve a very unpleasant customer. He was demanding, hostile and rude to me. At one point I was so infuriated at his behavior that I went into the kitchen to vent to my husband. I pointed out the customer and my husband was shocked, stating that he knew the man personally and considered him a good guy. My husband walked out to the man's table to say hello, to find out if there were issues with his meal or the service (there weren't) and to introduce the two of us. My husband thought that perhaps we got off on the wrong foot.

Well, once the patron realized that I was the chef's wife, and NOT a "lowly" waitress, his demeanor toward me changed completely. He became pleasant, chatty and engaging. He actually stated, "If I knew you were not just a waitress and you were Bruce's wife, I never would have treated you that way. I am sorry." When he learned that I owned a consulting firm that specialized in placing professionals in his field, he nearly jumped from his chair! It turned out that he was actively searching for a new job.

Can you guess what transpired next?

To make a long story short, I found a great job for this once-rude customer. And believe me, before I cautiously sent him on that interview I gave him some advice. "Remember to treat the receptionist better than you treated me the night we first met, when you thought I was JUST a waitress and somehow beneath you. Your behavior toward her will speak volumes. Some hiring managers even ask the receptionists their opinions of job candidates before hiring them."

From that experience, forward, I made absolutely sure that all attendees understood WHY I restrict certain terms on nametags. In networking, passing judgment is a mistake. You never know who is in a position to help change your life for the better.

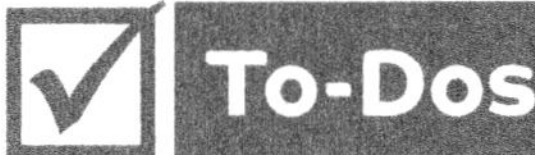

As an attendee, there are things you can do on your own to break the ice with your fellow Speed Networkers.

1. **TAKE PICTURES:** First, you need to create a good excuse for carrying the camera or using your smart phone camera: "I like to remember faces instead of names…I am writing a blog and want to post a photo… My company newsletter likes me to document unique networking events." No matter what you come up with, the simple act of taking the picture allows you to easily introduce yourself, learn peoples' names, and encourage collegiality. (And acting as unofficial photographer makes YOU memorable, too!)

2. **USE A CLASSIC HOOK:** Did you have trouble finding this place? Can you believe all the rain we're having? Are you keeping up with the latest news on (insert topic here)? These are just a few can't-miss ice-breakers. When all else fails, just reach out your hand and say, "Hi, I'm ____________."

3. **STAND NEAR THE FOOD:** "Have you tried the brownies?…Let me get you some utensils…Is this decaf or regular?" If you are looking for a safe spot to kick off a conversation, there's probably no better place to put yourself than in front of the food station. Just remember your table manners.

Zooming In For a Closer Look

We've just taken a broad overview of the typical Speed Networking event. Now, let's explore the different formats employed by Speed Networking event organizers.

There are three basic forms of Speed Networking:

1. Random Round Robin
2. Station-based
3. Group

Random Round Robin

For me, this is pure, unadulterated Speed Networking in its most organic form. This approach can work well for business as well as social functions and allows the participants to develop a broad, diverse sphere of influence. There is very little "manipulation" done on the part of the organizer to pre-assign matches, although organizers of this type of event do try to avoid introducing those attendees who are in competing businesses. For instance, if there were two residential mortgage brokers in attendance, they would be positioned so as NOT to meet during the event. However, if they were different types of mortgage brokers—a residential and a commercial broker, for example—I would want them to meet to perhaps explore a strategic partnership.

Basically, a sequence of one-on-one meetings takes place throughout the event. At my Speednetworx™ functions, attendees start off the evening seated in two facing rows. Pairs are separated by a tabletop, approximately two feet in width. This allows a comfortable distance for the pair to hear each other and take notes while still maintaining personal space. Note that the circle-in-circle formation is a popular alternative to the facing rows arrangement. This formation is shown in the graphic on the following page.

I stand at the end of the long table with one row of attendees to my left and one to my right. Before the Speed Networking begins, I explain the following five-step process to the attendees.

STEP 1: Prepare yourself mentally to deliver a concise Elevator Pitch and also prepare yourself to listen intently.

STEP 2: Those to my left will be the first to speak. Upon commencement, the first group of speakers will be given one minute to pitch. Meanwhile, those to my right will listen.

STEP 3: After one minute, I announce "Switch" and those to my left become the listeners while those to my right speak. Like the first group, they will have one minute to pitch.

STEP 4: After one minute, I announce "Share." At this point, each person has given their pitch and the pair is now free to discuss how they might work together to help each other. This is the time to ask questions, share business cards and offer assistance—remember, Karma!

STEP 5: After two minutes of sharing, a buzzer is sounded, commanding those to my left to move to the next seat in a predetermined, orderly formation. The row to my right remains seated.

Using this Speed Networking structure, attendees can generally meet between ten and twelve new contacts in an hour.

How It Works: Random Round Robin Speed Networking

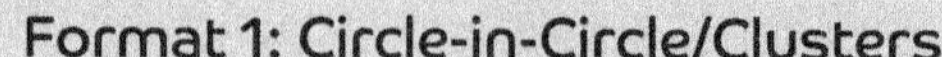

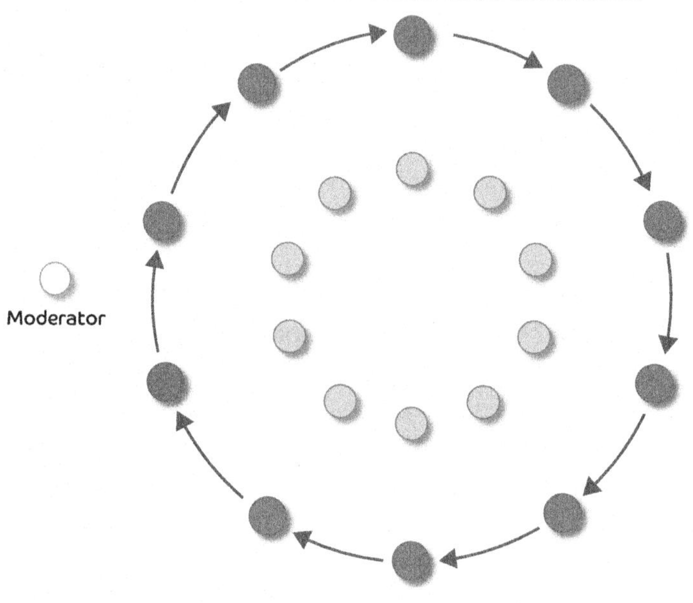

Using this format, event planners can quickly arrange chairs for impromptu Speed Networking. They may also choose to add horse shoe shaped tables.

Attendee stays seated

After each brief meeting, attendee moves to next seat

Format 2: Facing Rows/Tables

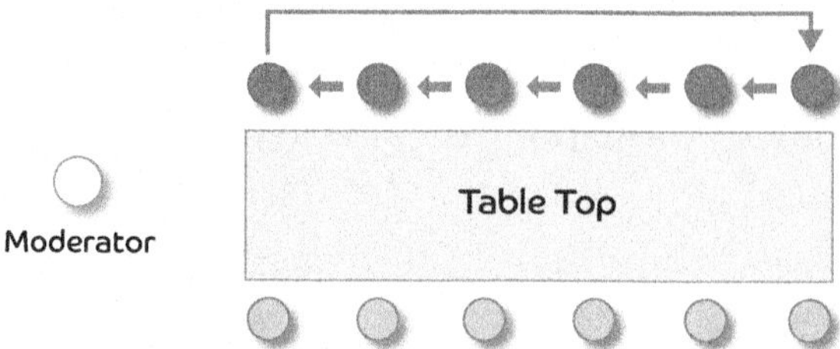

Using this Speed Networking format, participants are seated in two rows and separated by a tabletop, to allow note taking while maintaining personal space.

Attendee stays seated

After each brief meeting, attendee moves to next seat

Station-based Speed Networking

In Station-based Speed Networking, attendees are pre-matched electronically. In advance of the event, a questionnaire is distributed and the information provided is used to group participants based on their business title, industry and other qualifying data. Much like modern matchmaking, elaborate software finds mutual affinity among attendees and stations these "matches" together based on networking goals and areas of interest or specialization. Once attendees arrive at the event, they are directed to the appropriate station and the Speed Networking commences. The stations, again, can be set up as a circle in a circle, or facing rows.

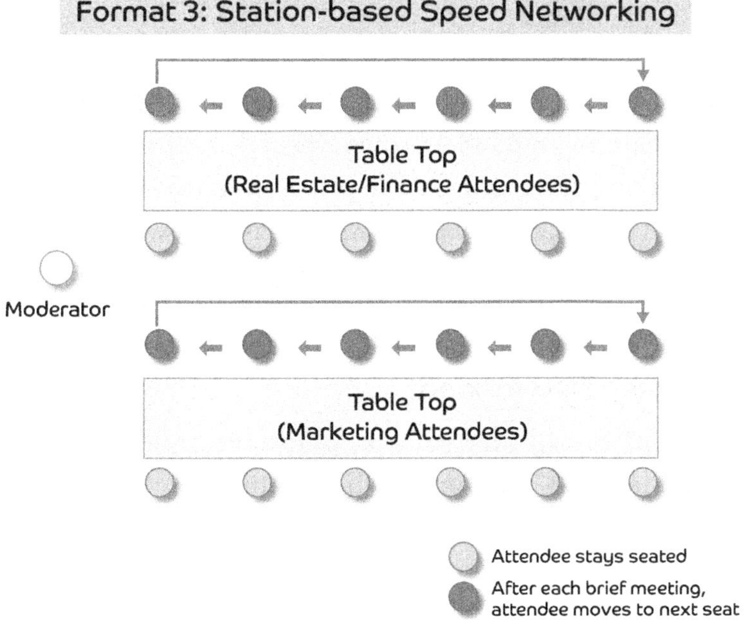

Similar to Format 2, however this Speed Networking format organizes attendees by various interests or specializations. *NOTE: At the end of any Speed Networking event, if time and headcount allow, a final round of speed networking can be added. This mini-round would accomplish two things: (1) it would allow those who were seated to meet each other, and (2) it would also allow the "movers" to meet each other. This way, all those who did not connect earlier would have an opportunity to meet.*

The Definition of "Bottleneck"

What is a bottleneck? In the dictionary, it is defined as "a place or stage in a process at which progress is impeded." In Speed Networking, it is defined as "CeeCee."

CeeCee (not her real name) came to one of my events last year. For some reason, she did not feel the need to follow the orderly process I outlined (and mentioned repeatedly) throughout the evening. After each of her brief meetings with other attendees, she completely ignored the buzzer, which commanded her and others to stand up and move to the next seat. While the people to her immediate right and left stood up and attempted to move on, she remained seated, determined to complete her discussion with her new acquaintance.

Because of her stubborn refusal to keep the flow moving, the evening's success was hindered. I was forced to confront her directly, ask her if there was a problem (there wasn't) and let her know that she was ruining the event for the other attendees. I explained to CeeCee that if Speed Networking rules aren't followed by everyone, no one can benefit from the experience.

Group Speed Networking

This form of Speed Networking allows attendees to meet in groups rather than one-on-one. Depending on the number in attendance, there may be anywhere from five to eight people at a table. Generally, a software program helps the event planner to maximize the number of introductions that can be made throughout the evening. In Group Speed Networking, each person at the table has a set amount of time to introduce himself. Once each person speaks for her allotted time, there is a brief period of free-flowing conversation before attendees move to the next predetermined table to meet the next group. There are benefits as well as drawbacks to this format.

Benefits: Obviously, introducing yourself over and over again, amid the background buzz and enthusiasm of the other networkers, can be tough on your throat. This format is less physically demanding because you are addressing a group rather than individuals. Also, the group format allows participants to meet many more people during the same time allotment. Attendees can come away from the event with dozens of new contacts.

"You never know who you'll meet, which connections may lead to your best business opportunities, and on what path a chance meeting might take you.

I have attended a number of Speednetworx™ events. I've met many good people and quality professionals—a few of those have led to great business opportunities. At one of these events I met a professional recruiter. We had coffee after the event and I asked her to introduce me to the decision maker at her firm who would benefit from my services. She agreed to do so and while I did meet with this person, we never conducted any business together.

However, she did introduce me to another professional in my field. (Ironically, she met this professional at a networking event!) This new contact introduced me to a prestigious firm in my field. This introduction eventually led to a job offer.

The moral of my story is to always keep an open mind when talking to other professionals at networking events. You never know what opportunities the introduction will lead to."

~ Ciro J. Giue, CPA
Consultant

Drawbacks: In the Group Speed Networking format, as in life, it is the squeaky wheel that gets the grease. Generally, the more gregarious participants in the group get the floor and those more introverted get to listen. The open exchange of this format is less structured than one-on-one Speed Networking.

What Speed Networking Is NOT

We've been covering the basics of what Speed Networking is all about; now let's discuss what it IS NOT. As mentioned at the beginning of the book, Speed Networking is NOT Speed Dating. And that bears repeating.

I've been attending and hosting Speed Networking events for years and it never ceases to amaze me; at every event there is at least one misguided person who is clearly focused on working a pick-up line, not an Elevator Pitch. Not only is this terribly distracting, but it is also uncomfortable for the others in attendance who must politely side-step the advances (which are sometimes subtle and other times blatant!). Those attending Speed Networking events are there for one thing and one thing only: to build their personal network. Speed Daters, you've got the wrong venue.

Another point worth clarifying: if you think Speed Networking is an opportunity for rapid-fire, hard selling, you are in the wrong place. A Speed Networking event is not the proper venue for winks and nods, back slaps and sleazy, insincere sales tactics. "Call me this week for a fifty percent discount opportunity" or "refer me and I'll give you a cut" are not appropriate suggestions to make at these events. Perhaps, down the road, you may find the opportunity to do business and extend special offers to your new contact. However, your initial meeting is very brief—just a few minutes—and certainly the time is best used to make a good impression. In the long run, your best efforts will lead to meaningful, long-lasting, give-and-get relationships.

"I paid $39 to come to tonight's event. I'm not happy with the results. I didn't get one new client; not even a prospect. This experience was useless. I would like my money back."

These are the words of a very misguided, first-time Speed Networker.

"Helen" wanted instant gratification. She wanted to take, not give. Helen completely missed the point of Networking Karma. She was looking at networking as a transaction.

I gave Helen her money back, and I gave her some good advice too. Networking is all about helping your contacts—going out of your way to make new relationships work. As mentioned in the Preface: *Your infinite potential, the very best person that you can be, may very well lie in the hands of another person; someone you have yet to meet.*

Isn't that reason enough to nurture every connection? After all, you never know where a new relationship might go. This is an enlightened perspective on networking. It is the opposite of transactional; it is transformational.

What about other forms of networking? Social media, for instance? Please, do not abandon other forms of networking! Speed Networking is NOT a replacement for other networking tools. The key to making Speed Networking work is to continue to develop and nurture the contacts you make over time.

LinkedIn and other online networking tools allow users to easily continue to build on the initial Speed Networking dialogue. They are the perfect sources for supplementing or enhancing your networking efforts. I use Speed Networking and LinkedIn in partnership to enhance my efforts to develop my sphere of influence. I'll discuss this in more detail in CHAPTER 11.

Speed Networking is also NOT about finding that one perfect client or opportunity. If you want to use it to its full potential, you cannot treat Speed Networking as a means to eliminate contacts. It is used to broaden your network by connecting with as many varied people as possible, even if it seems you have little in common with them. Remember Karma: the more people you can help, the more you will get in return.

There are other forms of face-to-face networking too, but they are NOT like Speed Networking.

Business cocktail mixers are very important to attend if you want exposure to others in your industry. The drawback of mixers is that they can be difficult to optimize. Frequently, attendees gravitate toward those they know and don't break out of their comfort zone to meet new faces. This is especially true of introverts who may not feel comfortable mingling and schmoozing.

Many folks have had proven success with business networking groups like BNI™ and Le Tip™, but again, they are NOT the same as Speed Networking. These organizations focus strictly on the bottom line; their referral networking platforms are transaction-based. Local Chambers of Commerce also provide opportunity for businesses to advance their interests and enhance local recognition. However, because they restrict membership based on locale, Chamber of Commerce groups have their limitations too.

Speed Networking facilitates relationship development and does not force the exchange of business favors. There is no membership or commitment of any kind. That being said, I do not want you, my reader, to think it is the "best" type of networking. They all have their pros and cons. And experts agree that none should be relied upon as a sole source for networking. Yes, my concept of Networking Karma can be applied to business networking groups (you give and receive tips and referrals); however they do not offer the same variety of interactions and over time these sources do dry up.

Who Speed Networks?

General Speed Networking events attract a variety of professionals from many different industries and disciplines. However, Speed Networking events can also be customized for specialized group networking opportunities. Speed Networking is very effective when attendees are in complimentary industries (e.g., real estate, mortgage, home inspectors); there are numerous ways to implement this format for success. Take a look!

- **STUDENTS/ALUMNI:** At any given university, you will find hundreds if not thousands of enthusiastic undergrads chomping at the bit for a post-graduation, entry-level job opportunity. On that same campus, there are powerful, influential alumni groups as well as educators who may be in a position to offer mentoring, recommendations, support, post-grad fellowships or even job placement assistance. Bringing these groups together for a two-hour networking event is a win-win.

- **INDUSTRY SPECIFIC:** My Speed Networking business recently planned an event for social media professionals. Programmers, writers, marketing experts, and web designers were all in attendance. Some were looking for work, others were looking to build their network and everyone came away with a better-equipped, trade-specific "tool box." The dynamic was exciting.

- **WOMEN'S GROUPS:** I hosted an event for an organization of women re-entering the work force. It was truly amazing to see the give and take of this empowering group of women, who were so ready, willing and able to help and be helped.

- **JOB FAIRS:** Anyone who has attended a job fair knows that they can be simultaneously boring and overwhelming. The structure of a Speed Networking event is perfectly suited to bringing together job hunters and recruiters. The organization of these events is quite intensive, but the payoff is undeniable. Matching recruiters with numerous, prequalified candidates within a set time frame makes for a very efficient pre-interview process. Unlike regular job fairs, my firm's SpeedHire™ events are FREE and FUN!

- **IN-HOUSE MIXERS:** One of the easiest and most successful ways to build employee engagement is through good, old-fashioned, face-to-face communication. Not just the kind that occurs between employer and employee; certainly this is vital. I'm talking about the kind of communication that goes on between coworkers throughout an organization. Inter-office Speed Networking is a growing trend that allows coworkers to meet each other and gain a fuller understanding of what they do in relation to others.

  In-house mixers also allow for more open communication, which helps groups interact more harmoniously. Camps, assisted-living facilities and college dorms are also great venues for in-house Speed Networking mixers.

- **COMMUNITY FUNCTIONS:** From the PTA kick-off meeting to the church social, from school orientations to vendor showcases, Speed Networking has possibilities for expansive application.

Chapter 4

SPEED NETWORKING AND LIFE

"It is hard to fail, but it is worse never to have tried to succeed."
~ Theodore Roosevelt

Let's delve below the surface for a moment, and explore the less tangible benefits to Speed Networking (or any networking for that matter). My philosophical viewpoint on networking is deep. It is based on life and change.

It's cliché but true: the only constant in life is change. We change schools, jobs, locations and (sometimes) marital status throughout our lives. And these transitions can be very trying on our emotions. The ability to use these opportunities as tools to improve our lives is a vital skill for us all. The secret to reducing stress and getting maximum satisfaction comes with developing the skills we need to successfully manage life changes. Whether bouncing back from financial ruin, divorce or illness, utilizing these necessary skills can turn stumbling blocks into stepping stones.

What are these life skills? Well, we have all heard that the most successful people master the art of goal setting. Staying organized is another important aspect to managing our lives and the changes that come about. Thinking in a positive manner is also vital to living fully. And of course, relationship development; that's where Speed Networking comes in.

Speed Networking is a unique form of relationship management that allows you to develop a large and positive sphere of influence. The relationships you make and nurture help you increase your productivity, enhance your career, and enrich your life in many ways.

Life=the people you meet + what you create together

This brilliant equation was penned by Christine Comaford-Lynch. Her book, *Rules for Renegades: How To Make More Money, Rock Your Career and Revel in Your Individuality*, explores her unbelievable success story and shares her off-beat rules and unconventional life lessons. Here are her "learn to love networking" essentials.

To-Dos

1. **EQUALIZE YOURSELF WITH OTHERS:** Just because people are powerful, rich or famous does not mean they are better than you. Practice equalizing yourself with others; remembering this will enable you to more comfortably interact with others.

2. **BUILD YOUR NETWORKING MOMENTUM:** Talk to people…all the time: in line at the store, at the

salon, on an airplane. Not sure how to start? Offer a compliment.

3. **ROLODEX DIP:** Flip through your contact database until you find a name that makes you smile. Then call that person up just to see how he or she is. Your contact will be surprised and delighted.

4. **DAILY APPRECIATION:** Appreciate at least one person daily. I often do this via email so I can be thorough. You can also express appreciation over the phone or in person. Simply tell others how much you appreciate who they are, what they do, whatever about them moves you.

5. **SENSEI OF THE DAY:** Each day I pick a sensei, a teacher. This is someone who has taught me a lesson or reminded me of something important in life … acknowledge that there is much to learn and that you are being offered valuable lessons constantly.

When Should You Speed Network?

"The biggest mistake new networkers make is going out and trying to start networking when they NEED a job. I believe networking at the time of NEED is too late. Networking is a lifestyle!"

~ Jill Neff, Buck Consultants, Compensation Director

Speed Networking Is Forever

As previously mentioned, the only constant in life is change. And because our lives are always changing, we constantly need to work on our relationships and the skills that help us to develop them to their full potential. Frequently, people ignore their networking until there is a need. This is especially true of those trying to find a new job.

In a 2009 survey conducted by outplacement consultants Challenger, Gray & Christmas, Inc., human resources executives were asked to rate the effectiveness of various job-search methods on a scale of one (least effective) to five (most effective). Networking averaged a 3.98. About half (forty-eight percent) of the respondents gave networking the highest effectiveness rating of five. I have shared this statistic with hundreds of job seekers and they all respond the same way: "I should have been developing a network of contacts while I was still employed...."

How Does Your Garden Grow?

Here is an analogy I share with my networking groups: *Building your network is like planting a garden.*

In order to get big, beautiful flowers or delicious produce from your garden, not only must you plant seeds (in the earth as well as in the minds of your prospective contact); you must also nurture your growing plant as you would your new relationship. In every garden, some seeds will be more bountiful than others. And the same goes for your network. If the conditions are right and you treat the new growth with care, you will get much pleasure from your efforts.

You wouldn't wait for your plants to die to water them, would you? Then why would you wait for a career crisis to nurture and grow your own personal network?

Your network is like a growing crop. Scrambling to build up contacts at a desperate time is like trying to bring a dying plant back to life. It's always easier to reach out to an established circle of supportive contacts. Certainly, having a healthy network in place is vital to growing your career continuously.

But this reasoning can extend to virtually every aspect of life. By nurturing your network daily—forging relationships, sharing information and connecting with people who all have a common objective and a generous spirit—your life goals can be reached more effectively. And like adding new plants to your garden, it is important to continually reach out to new people to gain fresh perspective, new information, and ideas that can be shared and used.

Are You Ready to Speed Network?

Take a moment now to examine your life. Couldn't you benefit from a fuller, deeper pool of contacts and connections? After all, the more positive, mutually beneficial relationships you develop, the more support you will have when you need it. As you have probably concluded by now, not everything you want to accomplish in your life is within your power to complete alone—no matter how self-sufficient you are. Knowledge is power, and quite often it is your network of contacts that holds the knowledge you need to help you succeed.

So, if you believe it is time to take control and fulfill your potential, start serving others today! Expand your influence and plot out the life that you want. You can do it and Speed Networking can help!

Part II
CONNECT

Chapter 5

THE FIRST IMPRESSION

"The answer is that we are not helpless in the face of our first impressions. They may bubble up from the unconscious—from behind a locked door inside of our brain—but just because something is outside of awareness doesn't mean it's outside of control."

~ Malcolm Gladwell

Nothing can take the place of good old-fashioned, face-to-face communication. After all, the written word can allow us to exaggerate, argue, and basically express ourselves in any number of extreme ways. Anyone can hide behind a glitzy website, well-written sales pitch or resume; however, when we meet face-to-face, our true selves emerge as we make and read expressions, speak honestly, connect fully and truly understand people on a more personal level.

Bottom line: face-to-face is the most honest way to start a new relationship and Speed Networking provides all attendees with the opportunity to connect in what is undeniably the best way.

How long does it take you to form a first impression?

According to a study by Michael Sunnafrank of University of Minnesota and Artemio Ramirez Jr. of Ohio State University, it can take as little as three minutes to determine how a relationship will progress. In a survey of one hundred and sixty-four college freshmen, the two professors found that first impressions had a strong influence on future relationships.

Sunnafrank and Ramirez's findings differ with previous research, which assumed that it takes days, even weeks, to determine how a relationship will progress. "We found that if two people take an immediate liking to each other, the relationship will most likely grow over time. It happens very rapidly," said Sunnafrank, lead author of a report on the research published in the *Journal of Social and Personal Relationships.*

Various studies and experts have weighed in on this issue. And although the time frame varies in the research, all can agree that our personal reactions to most situations are based on our past experiences, while our first impressions affect how we will interact with a new acquaintance going forward.

Given this knowledge, we need to think about how we present ourselves during Speed Networking (and throughout life). Everything from the clothes we wear, to the tone of our voice, to the way we shake hands has an impact. And while no one should EVER compromise their individuality, I believe you can become a better version of yourself with some self-reflection and awareness.

Your Personal Brand

In the corporate world, businesses invest time, energy and money to define the elements that make their products or services unique. They build brands! I'm not talking about cool logos or catchy taglines; I'm talking about deep-seated ideas that take root in every aspect of the company's business activities. Like brands in the corporate world, we can all manage the elements that go into our OWN brand—our PERSONAL BRAND.

No matter your line of work or station in life, you need to recognize your individuality. After all, it's easy to be like everyone else. But it's the things that make you different which allow you to stand out in a crowd and make first impressions last.

Let's explore how to develop a personal brand. Here we take some cues from some of the most successful brands on earth.

1. **BE MEMORABLE:** Memorable people remain fresh in our thoughts and in our conversations, long after our experiences with them are over. Some of the most notable personal brands have been built on a person's interesting and unique characteristics. For example, when you hear "You're Fired!," Donald Trump comes quickly to mind. The strength of his personal brand has endured because he has created a formula for success unlike any other mogul in his industry. Mr. Trump always speaks his mind in a hard-hitting, no-holds-barred style that gives him an air of confidence and dominance. His appearance is also unforgettable—from his honey-colored, combed-over head to his rich, Italian leather-clad feet,

The Donald always looks like...The Donald! Love him or hate him, you won't soon forget him.

What can you do to make your personal brand unforgettable?

2. **BE CONSISTENT:** Martha Stewart has her eye for quality and "good taste." Howard Stern has his outrageous antics. These are the consistent elements that make some of the world's hottest personal brands powerful. Humans crave continuity and reliability and the best brands are built on expectations being met, every time. Is your personal brand, your image and everything you do consistent? From the way you dress, to the way you answer the phone, to the way you promote yourself, your personal brand needs to measure up to previously set expectations every time!

3. **BE AUTHENTIC:** In business and in life, you need to stand for something and deliver without exception. This requires some serious soul searching. Do you know who you truly are? Do your words match your deeds—every time? If not, your personal brand can suffer.

   One of my role models is Richard Branson, the British tycoon, philanthropist and adventurer. I've followed his career for years, read his books and studied his success formula. Upon close reflection, I've come to the realization that Mr. Branson's very full life is a result of his personal authenticity.

   Several years ago I learned this first-hand when I visited Branson's Virgin offices. As I entered the building I was charmed to see Mr. Branson's unique business style and mindset. I'll never forget the tie rack with instructions for tie wearers to "Leave your tie at the door." Branson believes that one's contributions rather than one's "uniform" speak for themselves, as evidenced by the clever office décor. From his bold business moves, to his love of risky sports, to his brave rescue flight into Iraq at the brink of the Gulf War, Branson's courage in business and in life has never waned or seemed insincere.

Chameleons take note! It's hard to maintain a strong personal brand if your authenticity is fleeting. In networking and in life, you can't be afraid of being different, especially when your differentiation is grounded in authenticity and goes to the core of who you are.

Chapter 6
IMAGE

"Without deviation from the norm, progress is not possible."
~ Frank Zappa

Wardrobe

I like to think of myself as open-minded, a free thinker. For as long as I can remember, the words "this is just how it's done" have been unacceptable to me. As a kid, I questioned why there were so many seemingly silly "rules" that people had to follow. I'm not talking about laws, just societal norms that are put upon us.

This confusion induced a lot of angst and frustration in my teenage years. I was ME and I was rejecting the labels that were being put on me. I simply could not accept being a certain way simply because "this is how it's done."

So during my late teen years and beyond, I connected with like-minded friends: kids and young adults who were in touch with themselves and weren't afraid to question all of the intolerance for individuality.

I evolved into a different look; some may have called me "Goth." I hated the label (really despised the idea of labeling anyone.) This was how I expressed myself; I was just being an individual.

Was I part of a cult? A Satanist? A dark, depressed, angry mystic? Absolutely not! That is the typical stereotype of a subculture I did not identify with. I was simply connected with and accepted by a group of like-minded people who were nonjudgmental, intelligent and (believe it or not) had a great sense of humor. They didn't mind laughing at themselves.

Did I wear black clothes, white face, dark makeup and listen to loud music? You bet! It was one of the most amazing, eye-opening periods of my life. I met some fascinating people and discussed some deep and meaningful topics. I wasn't trying to shock or antagonize the mainstream around me. I was just trying to march to the beat of my own drum and find myself.

But I have also learned from my earlier experiences that people's perceptions are also their realities. I clearly remember being asked to leave restaurants in New York City because of the way I used to look. Conclusions were drawn about me; to the observer I wasn't a straight-A student with a scholarship to NYU. I was a freak, a heathen, an undesirable. All of these judgments were based solely on my appearance. It bothered me that people could be so shallow and judgmental, but it didn't stop me from being me.

This early experience demonstrates the reality of human perception and how it affects opinion. It's a fact: people make quick judgments based on how others look. Sometimes, it's like love at first sight—eyes connect and a positive attraction occurs without a word being spoken. However, when someone's appearance does not make others comfortable, just the opposite can happen.

Simply put, people want to feel comfortable and safe with those with whom they associate—including friends, business associates and clients.

As an adult, I have found a way to strike the perfect balance: Sustaining the integrity of my personal image—staying true to myself—while simultaneously projecting how I want to be perceived at networking, in business and in life.

While I will always favor the color black and prefer an edgier look, I do occasionally need to dress like a CEO. Knowing this, I've spent a lot of time developing a wardrobe that includes several black dresses, platform boots and offbeat accessories. These carefully selected pieces allow me to live by my own rules—to express myself without totally conforming.

Your appearance sends a powerful message. It creates an impression and sets expectations. In other words, the way you look is an extension of your personal brand.

To-Dos

Before venturing out to your next networking event, here is some advice from Suze Yalof Schwartz, former Executive Fashion Editor-at-Large of *Glamour Magazine.* She has been an internationally recognized stylist and TV personality and is well known in the fashion industry for her chic, accessible style. On the next page, she shares what's hot and what's not when it comes to developing your wardrobe for most corporate events and making the very best of that vital first impression. While these tips may not resonate with every reader, they are the gold standards for a play-it safe, classic dress-for-success strategy.

1. **SUPERCHARGE YOUR STYLE:** Think about your goals in life and how you should look when you achieve them. Don't wait to attain that "look"—get it NOW!

2. **LITTLE OVERSIGHTS = BIG FAUX PAS:** Overlooking the smallest details—frayed handbag straps, chipped nail polish, scuffed shoes, an errant bra strap—can lead to misjudgments about who you are and what you stand for. Sweat the small stuff.

3. **STEER CLEAR OF OVER-ACCESSORIZING:** Rather than loading on the accessories and then taking "one piece off," my advice is to wear just one big statement piece. It should add interest and personality without detracting from your appearance.

4. **GET THE RIGHT FIT:** Often overlooked but vitally important to your style and your comfort, alterations should not be optional. After all, a perfectly tailored, mid-priced outfit trumps ill-fitting designer duds, every time.

5. **BE ON THE READY:** Everyone should have a last minute, go-to, no-fail networking outfit. Ladies can't go wrong with a smart black dress and heels, between two and four inches in height. Men do best in a dark suit or slacks with a crisp white shirt. (And always have a tie handy—just in case!) In networking, jeans are a no-no.

If these guidelines seem confining—if you want to network by *your own rules and nobody else's*—here's some good news. A 2014 study by Harvard University doctoral student Silvia Bellezza and assistant professors Francesca Gino and Anat Keinan revealed that those who go out on a limb with their business wardrobe could appear more successful to others. According to Bellezza, "nonconformity can be perceived as admirable behavior that reflects high levels of autonomy and control. Deviating from the norm signals freedom and autonomy from the pressure to conform, and thus can fuel positive inferences in the eyes of others." The study is entitled, "The Red Sneaker Effect."

While I would never suggest that you be different for the sake of being different, if you want to express your own style, I say go for it! Try on a pair of striking eyeglasses, a red tie, an accessory that reflects your uniqueness. Anything that makes you memorable and distinctive is, in my opinion, totally acceptable. I think Mark Zuckerberg would agree!

Body Language

Stand up straight. Shoulders back. Arms at your sides. Head held tall. No, this isn't a military exercise. It's all about body language. You've heard it before but it bears repeating: you can speak volumes without uttering a word. Are you guarded in your interactions? Are you truly interested in what the other person is saying? Do you exude confidence? Those meeting you for the first time will make these judgments by reading your body language.

Recently, "Tracey" attended her first Speed Networking event. She owned a dog training business and had worked with animals for over twenty years. I was struck by the disconnect between her personal presentation and her occupation. You see, she had impeccable posture, a long straight back and regal neck. She carried herself throughout the event with her head held high. I was fascinated that this very proper-looking woman had a career working with four-legged clients. But when she started speaking, I was reassured by her knowledgeable insight regarding the canine world. A week later, I was in touch with her. Although her fees seemed quite high, I did engage her business services. I think there was something about her graceful air and confident demeanor that made me comfortable with her upscale fees. I firmly believe that her body language helped earn her place in the high-end pet care industry.

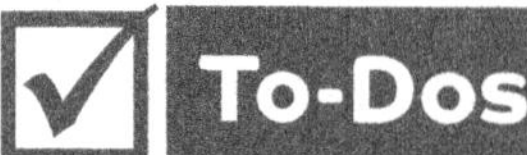

To-Dos

Mark Bowden is a world-renowned body language expert and creator of TruthPlane, a communication and presentation training tool used by Fortune 500 companies, CEOs and world leaders. Mark's book *Winning Body Language* (McGraw Hill, 2010) explores the overwhelming role played by nonverbal communication when we speak to an audience.

Here are ten To-Dos from Mark's book on how to use body language to your advantage.

1. **PUT YOUR BODY ON DISPLAY:** When speaking, step away from impediments; if sitting, pull your chair back from the table—in short, display more of your body. Your audience's instinctual "reptilian" brain and emotional "limbic" brain need to see your body to

decide what they think your intentions and feelings are towards them. The less you show, the more they make those feelings and intentions up, and tend to default towards the negative.

2. **SPEAK FROM YOUR BELLY:** Place your hands in what is called the TruthPlane, the horizontal plane that extends 180 degrees out of your navel area, to display a sense that you can be trusted. Bringing the audience's unconscious attention to this very vulnerable area of your body makes them feel like you are very confident; and by assuming this physicality, you will feel confident too.

3. **SHOW YOUR HANDS:** Show your palms open with nothing in your hands to let others know that you mean no harm and are speaking for their benefit. This gesture is universally recognized as "friendly."

4. **INVITE THE AUDIENCE IN:** When someone else is speaking, keep your hands in the TruthPlane so that they understand you are open to what they say. By making small "inviting" gestures in towards you, you give the feeling that you want to know more from them.

5. **RAISE THE BAR ON ENERGY:** Show your listener you are excited by the idea you are speaking about by raising your hands to chest level, known as The PassionPlane. This sends your own heart rate, breathing and blood pressure up; and your listener will mirror this physical reaction by getting excited and passionate with you.

6. **HANG OUT...CHECK OUT:** Avoid hanging your hands down by your side when giving important messages. When you are still, your brain gets messages to slow down breathing and heart rates, and your voice will take on a depressing or sleepy downward intonation. Again, your audience will mirror this action—and that's how to put them to sleep!

7. **ATTRACT THE RIGHT PEOPLE:** Keep your gestures symmetrical. The brain understands symmetry in the body more easily than asymmetry, and we find symmetry more attractive. In nature, symmetry is seen as an indicator of a healthy gene pool.

8. **BETTER TO REVEAL THAN CONCEAL:** Avoid having your hands at mouth level when speaking, for example when sitting at a table with your chin in your hands. We lip read more than we think, and when the picture of the words is taken away it becomes harder to verify the language.

9. **MOVE COMPLEX TO CLEAR:** When giving a complex message, avoid complex movement, especially in the fingers—no fiddling erratically with your pen! It is hard for the brain to decode complex verbal language when it is concentrating on complex nonverbal behavior. Your audience will stop listening while they try to understand what you are doing and what it means.

10. **STOP READING AND START LEADING:** Stop trying to read other people's body language consciously! Generally, most of us stand little more than a 50/50

chance of getting it right. While we can often tell the feeling, we cannot tell the cause of the feeling, and easily jump to negative conclusions.

Facial Expressions

In 2009, the University of Glasgow's Department of Psychology conducted a study led by Professor Philippe Schyns. Their findings: the brain requires just two hundred milliseconds to collect most of the data needed from a facial expression in order to decipher a person's emotional state. Although the pace of a Speed Networking event is lightning-fast, there is still plenty of time for your fellow attendees to decode your expressions and judge you accordingly.

Happy? Fearful? Surprised? Disgusted? Angry or sad? No matter how you feel, your expression tells the world. Facial expressions are a key form of nonverbal communication and their role in person-to-person communication is substantial. Your expressions provide commentary to the words you use (or the words you hear), and understanding and managing your expressions is important for successful interpersonal communication.

Many times, people aren't even aware of the expressions beaming across their face. Although most professionals choose to keep their personal emotions to themselves, very often they expose their feelings through their expressions without meaning to, or wanting to. This is especially true of the unemployed and/or those looking for an opportunity. It can be fairly easy to spot the person who's most desperate—the clenched teeth, serious demeanor and sweaty brow are dead giveaways.

We've all had the experience of approaching someone who has a scowl on his face. It immediately puts us on the defensive. A word of advice I share with all new Speed Networkers: smile. A smile is an invitation to connect. It allows access, calms nerves and sends a signal that says, "Please approach." As Victor Borge once said, "A smile is the shortest distance between two people."

Grooming and Good Health Habits

Your personal habits affect those around you. Good hygiene reduces the spread of illness, builds confidence, and enhances your chances for overall personal and professional success. However, you would be amazed at the number of people who show up to networking events with food in their teeth, body or cigarette odor, unkempt hair and dirty fingernails.

According to the Bureau of Labor Statistics data on Personal Care Activities in 2012, the civilian population spent on average, about forty-five minutes per weekday on grooming and health-related self-care activities. That's less than one hour a day to bathe, apply beauty and hygiene products, style hair, brush teeth and get dressed. Are you spending less than this amount of time each day to get yourself together? If so, you may want to question if you are doing all you can to take care of your personal grooming and health habits. After all, if people can't care for themselves, how can they be expected to care for and nurture their life, their business and their contacts?

Chapter 7

THE ELEVATOR PITCH

"The story of the human race is the story of men and women selling themselves short."

~ Abraham Maslow

WE'VE DISCUSSED THE ROLES your wardrobe, body language, facial expressions and grooming play in making a good first impression. Now it's time to explore the verbal elements that come into play. The top of the list? Your "Elevator Pitch." Quite simply, an Elevator Pitch is a concise, carefully planned and well-practiced description about what you do. It's called an Elevator Pitch because you should be able to deliver the information in the time it takes to ride an elevator from the top floor to the bottom of a tall building. Most successful networkers have found a way to deliver their pitch in one minute or less, depending on the circumstances.

If you submit the term "Elevator Pitch" to the Google search engine, you will get literally thousands of links to explore. YouTube videos. How-tos. Step-by-step directions. Pros and cons. Dos and don'ts. There's an abundance of self-proclaimed experts posting advice galore on this subject. The reason the web is crammed with all of this insight, wisdom and information is clear. Virtually everyone, at one time or another, needs a succinct, eloquent and compelling way to "pitch" their product, service—even themselves!

It's not enough to create your Elevator Pitch. Every single person interested in building a network of contacts should have their pitch practiced and perfected.

The Elevator Pitch is an absolute necessity for Speed Networking. It's required to connect when faced with a limited amount of time and it's certainly required to maximize impact and memorability. An Elevator Pitch can help you make the most of every Speed Networking situation—it will certainly make the entire experience much easier and more productive.

Do you turn red, get flustered or tongue tied when talking about yourself? All the more reason to create a compelling Elevator Pitch. Putting time into the development of your pitch will take a lot of stress out of many situations, especially networking.

Your pitch's message should be simple and clear. A good rule of thumb: your pitch should resonate equally with a ten-year-old child or a seventy-five-year-old grandmother. In other words, it should have universal appeal. After all, if your listener doesn't "get it," how can he or she advocate for you, consider you for a job or refer you to others?

Now that you have the basic overview of what an Elevator Pitch is, let's talk about what an Elevator Pitch IS NOT.

An Elevator Pitch is never:

- A sales pitch
- A verbal resume

- A deal-closer
- An interview

Remember, if you only have a minute to state what it is you do, you'll simply want to pique someone's interest enough for that person to ask you for a follow-up to the conversation.

Creating Your Elevator Pitch

With little time to make an impression, your Elevator Pitch must spark a need, relate to your new contact, and compel that new contact to request more information about you and your product or service. Therefore, your successful pitch must include:

- A mention of your product or service, without going into granular detail.
- The target market of your product or service.
- The benefits that you, your product or services provide.
- An engaging comment or question to draw your audience into a fuller conversation.

And if time allows, ADD the following:

- An interesting case study that portrays exactly how you or your company helps people.
- Your background and related accomplishments.
- Your competition and the competitive advantage you offer.
- What you need your new contact to do; ultimately this call-to-action should help move your relationship forward.

Your pitch should be no longer than two hundred words; that's about sixty seconds worth of conversation. You will also need a powerful "hook" at the beginning of your pitch: an idea that will pique your audience's interest and make them want to hear more. A well-conceived question works well here.

Your pitch also needs to be impassioned; your enthusiasm must come through in the words and the delivery. And finally, you should end your pitch with a request. Ask for something in order to continue the dialogue. Try setting up a meeting. Ask your new contact to visit your website. Request a mailing address to send samples. *This is the most vital part of your initial contact; it's where you open the door to future conversations.*

Once you have found a concise treatment for the points above, you can start to finesse the ideas into a relaxed, conversational introduction that involves the listener and compels her to take action. That is the key!

Practice Makes Perfect

Crafting the ultimate Elevator Pitch may sound easy, but it isn't. Because of the brevity of the message, every word must count. Once you use the guidelines I've provided here and write every point down; read it and edit it. Then edit it again. And again. When it looks good on paper, read it out loud and listen. Is there a natural cadence to your pitch? Are the words easy to form and speak? Are you covering all of the important points? Is your passion and energy coming through?

Using the video camera on your computer, record yourself as you practice your pitch. Play it back and examine it critically. If you were the listener, would your words inspire action? What about your body language? Are you relaxed or tense?

Recite your pitch to your family, practice it in the shower, speak to your dog! Play around with the words until they sound conversational, friendly and natural; it takes work to perfect your pitch.

One sure-fire approach to acquiring all of the skills necessary to deliver a polished pitch is to actually immerse yourself in the Speed Networking environment. That's right! Like on-the-job training, Speed Networking allows you to get the very best training for the development and perfection of your "Elevator Pitch." The repetitive nature of the event ensures that you will get ample opportunity to try out your pitch and collect feedback on your performance (by reading your partner's body language and interest level). Speed Networking also allows you to study the successful skills of the more experienced networkers, and discover different ways you can tailor and tweak your pitch to your varied audience.

"When I attended my first Speed Networking event in June of 2011, I had recently looked at it as a chance to perfect my 'pitch' in front of like-minded business people.

The Speed Networking event started out with a small dinner. Afterward, the host distributed numbers and asked us to sit in assigned seats. And then, forced to sit across from entrepreneurs and business people, one-to-one, in a structured, time-limited environment, I was able to give my 'pitch' over and over again, trying different methods of introduction and description. I was also able to hear how others introduced their business, which assisted me in developing my own style.

By the end of the night, I felt much more comfortable with my 'pitch' and networking in general. And to add to my self-esteem, the next week I was contacted by an executive coach I had met at the event, asking me if I would be interested in partnering with her on several opportunities."

~ Jesse Broome, Online Marketing and Business Consultant

Elevator Pitch Dos and Don'ts

Your Elevator Pitch should always be focused on the needs of the person you are speaking with. If your time is limited (as in a Speed Networking event), your pitch needs to be hard-hitting and concise.

DO try it like this:

"Hi. I'm Gail Tolstoi-Miller. My company, Consultnetworx™, partners with organizations to help them hire the very best temporary and full-time talent in a number of specialized corporate areas. We support our clients' growth by identifying talent that's perfectly matched to their corporate culture and their needs. We do this by taking the time to assess clients' organizations and by exploring what hard and soft skills they require for each open position. We also save our clients time and money by identifying temporary talent quickly and shouldering the burden of all insurance and payroll costs associated with hiring consultants.

What have been some of your recent workforce challenges?"

Never make your Elevator Pitch an excuse to brag about your accomplishments. A BIG DON'T:

"Hi. I'm Gail Tolstoi-Miller; I am CEO of Consultnetworx™, a national consulting firm specializing in Human Resources, Manufacturing, Pharmaceutical, Corporate Support, Sales and Finance. Before starting my business, I was a very successful corporate HR executive. Within three years of branching out on my own, I won three very prestigious industry awards, quadrupled my recruiting staff, upgraded my corporate offices and built my client base with over a dozen Fortune 500s as well as several hot start-ups.

I would love to meet whomever is responsible for hiring decisions in your firm.

Could you give me their name and contact number?"

If your Elevator Pitch contains acronyms, techno-babble or industry jargon, it may be lost on your fellow Speed Networkers. Don't wait for their eyes to glaze over during your pitch. Take a look at this comparison below.

DO simplify complex features and functions into a quick benefit-driven chat.

"Hi. I'm Linda Smith; I represent Solar Now Technologies.

When I meet people, I like to ask them this question: Do you know the two biggest complaints of American consumers?

Well, the first is the rising cost of energy and the second is falling personal income.

My company helps home owners and business owners with both of these concerns. Our customers save hundreds and sometimes thousands of dollars a month by creating their OWN *energy from the sun.*

We are the leading solar panels installers in the region. And we're very busy. Right now we have eight hundred and eighty-nine installations in New Jersey alone.

In fact, I am a Solar Now customer. Last year twenty-two panels were mounted on my roof. I'm so happy that I made the decision to go Solar… my last utility bill was cut by eighty-five percent!

Solar Now offers a simple, no-money-down, turnkey solution that allows families and businesses to save for the things they truly care about.

This month we are offering free energy evaluations which show homeowners how to save more with solar panels. In fact, there are some little-known government rebates and grants available to offset the cost. Does that sound like something you'd like to learn more about?"

DON'T try to explain a complicated system in a one-minute Elevator Pitch.

"Hi. I'm Linda Smith; I represent Solar Now Technologies. My company installs solar panels on homes and office buildings.

As you may know, solar power involves small cells that absorb electromagnetic radiation, causing a chemical reaction and rapid electron movement. Because of the way the cells are layered, electrons are forced to move in one direction, causing direct current or DC. The DC is converted into something called alternating current or AC, which is useable energy for your home or office.

Would you be interested in learning more? I have a great PowerPoint presentation and my calendar is right here—we can set something up now. Also, I pay generous finders fees so if you can refer new business to me, you can make a nice amount of extra cash."

There's no doubt that when you have a well-honed pitch, you come across as confident and capable, and it makes others more inclined to trust you and consider you as a valuable contact. Besides allowing you to develop a rapport, a solid pitch will help you gather information about the people you meet and, most importantly, it will help you to be remembered!

Chapter 8

THE ART OF COMMUNICATION. THE ADVANTAGE OF COURTESY.

"Most people do not listen with the intent to understand; they listen with the intent to reply."
~ Stephen R. Covey

Our surroundings can offer us much in the way of personal growth and opportunity. However, most of us go through life on autopilot, too preoccupied or self-absorbed to appreciate all of the potential around us.

Using all of our senses helps us to observe more keenly, listen more intently, speak more accurately and converse with conscious cues. This heightened awareness of our surroundings allows us to tap into our best manners, which enhances every aspect of networking.

But awareness takes practice!

Remember, to develop and sustain your relationships with fellow networkers, be ever mindful. No doubt there will be times when you need to tap into your "play it safe" wisdom.

Here are smart strategies and social-savvy suggestions for communicating with care.

1. **KEEP A HANDLE ON THE HUMOR:** Perhaps you consider yourself a lighthearted, confident person who knows how to break the ice and add levity to business situations. That's great, as long as you recognize that there is a fine line to using humor effectively. While it's true that an amiable, witty person will be remembered as someone who can bolster a networking event, a wisecracking buffoon will be perceived as offensive, immature and irrelevant. Vulgarity, insults and profanity are unquestionably off-limits.

2. **KNOW THYSELF (AND THY AUDIENCE!):** Before networking, a bit of introspection is required. Ask yourself, "Is my personality extreme?" Whether you are assertive and hard-hitting, or very low key and bashful, mindfulness is key to succeeding in the networking environment and with your audience.

   For example, as I mentioned earlier, I'm an introvert by nature. While I can't (and don't want to) change who I am, I know that sitting in a corner at a networking event won't serve me well. So I put my best foot forward for that place and time—I interact in a more dynamic way, expanding my comfort zone ever so slightly. Similarly, a very high-strung individual can make a conscious decision to use personal tools (such as breathing exercises) to present more calmly. Socrates said it best. "Know Thyself."

3. **BE SENSITIVE TO SPACE:** While the range of some Americans' comfortable "personal space" is at least two feet in distance, other people feel very comfortable coming in closer. When uncertain, it is best to start off in your own personal comfort range and allow the other person to position herself where she feels best.

4. **DON'T TOUCH:** Keep your hands to yourself or risk ruining a first impression by insulting or shocking a fellow networker.

5. **WATCH YOUR GESTURES:** Giving the thumbs-up sign or waving are perfectly acceptable in the United States. In other cultures, they may be considered rude, evil or insulting. The bottom line, once again: Know your audience.

I've mentioned some cultural situations because we live, and network, in a global village. If you are going to networking events in other countries, or if you're invited to attend an event given by a foreign association or group, you should do your best to show respect and avoid embarrassment by reading up on regional etiquette, customs and manners.

Recognize and Use Cues in Conversation

You know that awkward feeling? When you get past the initial ice-breaker and then, crickets! The conversation hits a wall. You start fidgeting or staring at your shoes and hoping that someone comes along to rescue you from the painful silence.

There's no reason why anyone should let awkward communication skills betray their best intentions! By using "Connection Cues" you can work a room better and connect more powerfully. What's more, these essential tools transcend networking, helping in all aspects of life to command more positive interaction, attention and feedback.

SIX CAN'T MISS CONNECTION CUES

When used in networking situations, these smart small-talk tips will give you confidence and influence too.

1. Ask open-ended questions that can't be answered with "yes" or "no."
2. Pay a sincere compliment.
3. Ask your fellow networker to repeat or clarify something that seemed especially interesting or specific.
4. Compare personal interests.
5. Express your agreement when there's a common opinion.
6. Without being overly dramatic or controversial, express your feelings around a topic being discussed.

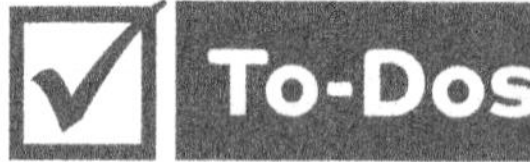

To-Dos

Here are some of my strategies for bringing a stalled conversation to its ending—without offending!

1. **INVITE YOUR FELLOW NETWORKER TO BE YOUR "WING MAN":** There's no need to abruptly end a conversation when you can subtly remove yourself. One way you might do this is to ask your new acquaintance

if she would like to join you at the buffet or come along to greet the guest speaker. Once you're on the move, there is a good chance an unexpected distraction will interfere with your conversation, or at the very least break the monotony.

2. **WAIT FOR A LULL OR A PAUSE IN THE CONVERSATION:** Take a cue from your conversation partner, who may begin to run out of material. When he uses terms such as, "so, anyway…" or "well…" and takes a long breath, this is a perfect time for you to subtly step back while offering a handshake. Using past tense pleasantries, simply say, "It was so nice to meet you, Mike. Will you excuse me?" If you choose warm words, display sincerity and a smile, this is a perfectly acceptable way to move on.

3. **MAKE A PREDETERMINED ESCAPE PLAN:** If you feel uncomfortable with the direct approach provided above, you will need an escape plan for such situations. Think about taking a bathroom break or moving on to another person you already know in attendance. Then, as the conversation winds down, say, "It was so nice to meet you, Mike. I have to make some arrangements with my colleague Jane. I'll catch up with you later." The key here is to follow through with the action you mentioned in your breakaway. If you take another path, you may hurt the feelings of your new acquaintance and appear rude.

4. **BRING OTHERS INTO THE FRAY:** If there are other attendees who may have some synergy with your

new acquaintance, make an introduction. Simply say, "Mike, there's someone I want you to meet who is also involved in the finance business." Once you introduce the two and they start to chat, just excuse yourself. You can say, "I'll leave you guys to chat. Let's catch up later."

Listening!

Let's imagine a very typical networking situation: You meet a new contact at a mixer or industry event, and he leaves a lasting impression, but for all the wrong reasons. He speaks a bit too fast and too loudly, interrupts constantly while you speak, one-ups every comment you make, provides unsolicited advice, and seems to require a great amount of attention. If you are a kind-hearted soul, perhaps you give this guy the benefit of the doubt; assuming he is either overly enthusiastic or just nervous about networking. But most people would not be so forgiving. Why? Because we all want to be heard.

By allowing someone to be heard, you are sending a nonverbal message that you value what that person feels or says. The art of "listening" is the most gracious element of communication. It requires us as listeners to be patient, generous and "in the moment," without having an agenda. Listening well comes naturally to some, but requires practice for others.

While what we say is important, it is equally important to put emphasis on how we listen. We tend to think of speaking as active and listening as passive, and speaking as the skill to hone while listening is automatic. Listening, though, is not passive, and it's not automatic. Careful listening is necessary for developing mutually beneficial, ongoing business relationships. Listening in a Speed Networking situation can be especially challenging, requiring careful focus in the midst of a fast-paced setting.

In any situation, you will increase your value by showing that you have the ability to pay attention, take in new information, and make others feel valued—all of which begin with listening.

☑ To-Dos

To gain expert advice on this vital subject, we enlisted the help of Linda Eve Diamond, the author of several books on listening, including *Rule #1: Stop Talking: A Guide to Listening.* Linda's tips are Speed Networking gold!

1. **STOP TALKING.** You can't multitask speaking and listening. If you're talking, you're not listening. This also applies to the talking you do inside your head, including thinking through what you will say while the other person is talking. If you have a carefully crafted Elevator Pitch, learn it well, and resist the urge to silently rehearse while others are talking. You will hear more of what others are saying, which may even help you deliver a more targeted message.

2. **FOCUS.** When someone is speaking, focus. When every movement in the room catches your eye, your lack of focus on the speaker is clear. Quiet your mind, even with the hurried situation around you, and focus your attention on listening in the moment. Careful listening requires focused attention.

3. **STAY CONNECTED.** Likewise, when you check every buzz, ring and ding on your phone, you don't come across as being interested in the speaker, which makes you less interesting too. If you're staying connected

with your social network and checking your incoming calls or instant messages, you're not connecting with the speaker. You can check your messages later, so give the speaker the message that you're paying attention.

4. **LISTEN CAREFULLY TO NAMES.** While you won't remember everyone's name in a Speed Networking situation, you may remember more than you'd expect by making an extra effort to listen when the name is said. Repeat the name when you are introduced, and try to use it a few times (as long as it sounds natural). If a name is unusual, double check that your pronunciation is correct. If the name on the person's business card is not spelled in a way that you would remember the pronunciation, jot your own phonetic spelling of the name on the back of the card so that you will remember how to pronounce it in the future.

5. **DON'T PRE-JUDGE ANYONE—EVER!** Everyone is unique and the process of labeling and making assumptions about people based on those labels short circuits the ability to listen. Any preconceived notion based on culture, politics or the myriad number of ways we define others, interferes with our hearing what each unique person has to offer. You may even meet someone you've heard is difficult in some way, but you don't really know the whole story of what transpired or whether you would have drawn the same conclusion. Any prejudgment limits your opportunities for mutually beneficial, enriching relationships.

6. **SUMMARIZE.** Two people can easily come away with completely different interpretations of a conversation, and

if four or five things are discussed in quick succession, one can easily be forgotten. If any follow-up actions are mentioned—sending or forwarding information, making a referral or introduction, scheduling a meeting, or just keeping in touch—a quick, friendly repetition before saying goodbye will make the agreement more memorable when you both walk away. (Of course, you'll want to jot yourself a reminder, too.) Summarizing shows that you are focused, listening and ready to take action.

Break Down Barriers and Be Curious

Giving voice to your thoughts is another vital area of personal awareness necessary for successful networking. As an introvert, I work hard every day to break down my internal barriers. I push beyond the MANY conversations I have in my head, and force myself to connect with others—to speak out loud and to act on my curiosity. When I do so, I am always amazed at the impact my outward voice has on my personal satisfaction and success.

Here's a perfect example of this: A few years ago, I was sitting in the airport, waiting for a delayed flight. I glanced up from the book I was reading and caught a glimpse of the woman sitting a few seats away. She was reading a popular human resources industry journal, one that I read myself. The voice in my head started asking the typical questions: "I wonder if she is a recruiter? Does she work for one of my clients? Have we met before?"

Rather than keeping my curiosity to myself, I spoke up.

"Hi, I noticed you are reading an HR magazine. Are you in HR?" I asked.

And guess what! That one simple question—two simple sentences—actually changed my life. My friendly inquiry led to a long conversation and an exchange of business cards. It turns out that my fellow passenger was the Human Resources Director of a large pharmaceutical company. She was impressed with my sourcing methods and my client list, and offered to connect me to her internal recruiters. I'm thrilled to tell you that this random meeting launched a long-standing and lucrative business partnership.

Understanding Your Personality Type

Are you an introvert or extrovert? How do you perceive and process information? Do you thrive in throngs or do you love being alone? Are you a thinker or a feeler? There are several insightful personality tests, which are designed to measure your personal tendencies. Where your results fall has a major influence on your personal networking strategies and successes.

In the resource section at the back of the book, you will find links to two leading questionnaires. Take these fun quizzes to gain a deeper understanding of yourself. You may also gain insight into how others perceive you.

Chapter 9
BUSINESS CARDS MEAN BUSINESS

"My Golden Rule of Networking is simple:
Don't keep score."
~ Harvey Mackay

There are many folks—networking purists—who feel that handing out business cards is phony: a forced formality that takes away from the pure engagement that comes from meeting and connecting with a new person. I don't agree with this at all. The traditional exchanging of business cards is an expected element of the networking experience. Tell someone "I forgot my card" or "I just ran out," and you risk souring that all-important first impression. What's worse, suggesting that your new contact "Google" you for your phone number is simply presumptuous and oozes of laziness.

Today, there's absolutely no excuse for not carrying a professional-looking business card. After all, there's a plethora of high quality, low cost online digital printers that allow you to customize the exact message and image you want to convey. Are you presenting yourself as entrepreneurial? Creative? Technical? All of these can be implied in the design choice you make.

As discussed earlier, your personal brand should be reflected in all of your communications, and that includes your business cards. The color, font, layout and any logos you use, add to the all-important first impression that you and your card exude.

Business Cards Hints and Tips

One design idea that is gaining in popularity is to print something unique on the back of your business card: a recipe, a list of your services, the periodic table, an inspiring quote, or anything relevant to your industry. You could also print a coupon code or an offer on the reverse of your card, giving it a perceived value and making it worth holding on to.

When conceiving your card, make sure your designer understands the concept of "negative space." In other words, leave some space around the main message so that the reader is not overwhelmed. The reader's eye should be drawn to, and naturally rest on, the most important elements of the card. Too much busy-ness is distracting and confusing. Another benefit of negative space: not only does it bring focus to your message, it also provides some clear space for your recipient to make a few notes.

"My business card will get sullied?" you ask. Yes. As much as we'd like our cards to be treated with respect and admired by recipients, people frequently jot down details as reminders of whom they met and any help they have agreed to offer.

Taking notes about each person you meet is a great first step in building a network. Make notes that will best jog your memory; think in terms of something you had in common with that person, what he or she looked like, where that person was from—details you think your new contact would be pleased to know you remembered are especially helpful when you reconnect. Showing you have an excellent memory is an impressive way to display your listening skills as well.

Another piece of advice: be sure to replace your cards immediately when your contact information changes. Receiving a business card with a scratched out phone number or address is an instant turn off.

Even yuckier is receiving a business card with a hair or a piece of gum stuck to it. Try keeping your business cards in a card holder. In fact, get a few card holders and keep them everywhere: your desk, your glove box, your purse. Always tuck a few emergency cards in your wallet too.

The Perfect Conversation Starter

As previously mentioned, at any networking event finding common ground can be nerve-wracking. All too often people resort to talking about the weather, the day's headlines or the always-common, "Have you been here before?" But every once in a while, an attendee catches my attention and stays in my memory because of an incredibly compelling business card.

Here are three creative approaches to business card design that have launched countless conversations, helping the card holders to connect with new contacts in interesting and unconventional ways.

1. **ADDED VALUE CARD:** Several years ago, a seasoned Executive Coach—let's call him "John Doe"—distributed

this business card at a networking function. He signed the back of it, handed it to me and made this offer: "FREE ADVICE FOR LIFE." What a great way to break the ice!

We spoke (mostly about me) and he made, and upheld, this promise: "If you ever need help navigating a professional challenge, please give me a call." Well, I have called him on two separate occasions (once, when an employee was challenging my authority and another, when my new boss asked me to lie to a client). He spent some time on the phone with me and provided valuable insight...FOR FREE.

Are you wondering how this gentleman makes a living while giving out these free cards? Well, his time with me translated into huge referral opportunities. I have given his name and phone number to at least fifteen friends and five of them hired him as their Executive Coach. Brilliant!

FREE ADVICE FOR LIFE

JOHN DOE
EXECUTIVE COACH

EMAIL:
WEB:

The Added Value Card.

2. **TOOL CARD:** Many business cards go directly from your hand to the garbage can. One of the best ways to ensure a long life for your card is to make it useful to the recipient.

   Broke Bike Alley bicycle technicians have had success with two different cards that act as handy tools. The first is a card made of rubber which can be used to patch a bike tire; the other is a metal die-cut "card" which allows the recipient to adjust a bike tire's bolts and spokes. (It even has a beer cap opener.) These useful cards are sure to stay in the wallets and on the minds of the recipients for quite a while. Even better, the "cards" may be passed on to others in need of Broke Bike Alley's services.

   Kudos to Rethink Creative Agency for these innovative business card concepts.

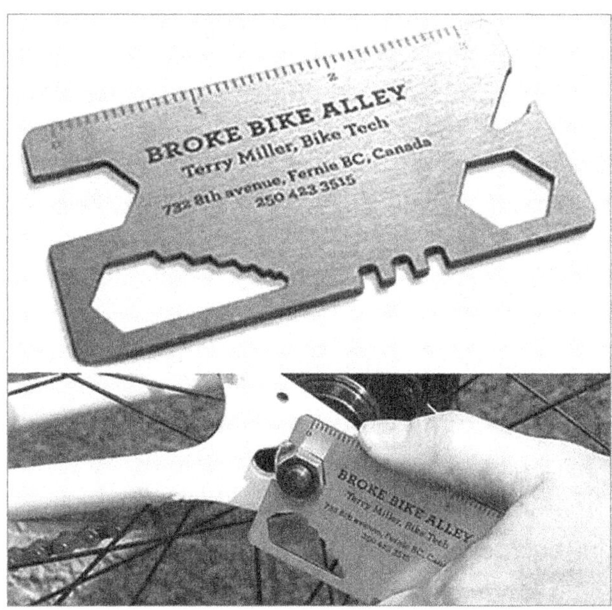

The Business Card as a Tool.

3. **INTERACTIVE CARD:** David Deasy's personal business card, a 2011 Platinum MarCom Award Winner, appeals to the senses with the touch-ability of letterpress—imperative since the user must interact with it to reveal the message: Great IDEAS and the designer (David DEASY) are synonymous. An image of the designer is also featured on the back of the card as an additional memory aid.

   The card succeeds in promoting the designer as one who doesn't simply make things look pretty, but knows how to propel a message further in a memorable way.

The Interactive Card.

Networking Cards: An Alternative

Are you planning a significant change of career direction? Would you rather NOT be associated with your business or company when making a first acquaintance at a networking event? In either case, your current business card may not be appropriate. Today, people are developing unique networking cards for specific goals. A career change, job search, entrepreneurial endeavor, fund raising effort or social outreach campaign are all scenarios requiring networking business cards.

Your networking business cards will ensure that:

- You make the appropriate impact on any important new contacts
- Your key "selling points" are on record for your new contact to see
- All of your relevant contact details are shared so that new contacts can connect with you

In a way, your networking business card acts like a mini résumé to remind your contact of who you are, what you have to offer, and how to get in touch with you.

In addition to the obvious elements like your name, email address and telephone numbers, be sure to include professional qualifications (CFA, MSW, Esq.) if relevant to your goal. If you have a personal website, a business website or even a LinkedIn URL, include it on your networking card. Don't be shy about printing your skills and achievements too.

Business Cards on the Cutting Edge

Of course, with the profusion of smart phone technology and networking apps, some folks are going paperless; rather than trading traditional business cards, they're exchanging electronic business information. In some industries, most notably the high-tech sector, the paper card is all but extinct. Numerous new high-tech products are making it possible to use mobile phones to transmit contact information.

As an added benefit, some of these apps and programs also tie in with contact management systems and even LinkedIn for seamless synching. To stay on the cutting edge of networking technology, check out Networking Karma's supplemental Tech Guide, for readers only. See Chapter 14 for complete details.

There are certainly great benefits to implementing these new technologies. First, using these systems allows you to "stand out" as an early adapter. And introducing the technology to curious folks at networking events is a great way to break the ice and be remembered. However, compatibility issues are a problem. And, in the realm of Speed Networking, valuable time is lost on explaining high-tech functions to your prospective new contact. Time must be used wisely and those precious moments needed to pitch yourself may be wasted on describing a new technology that ultimately will not help you find a real, meaningful connection.

Exchanging Business Cards

There is a gentle art to exchanging business cards, even in a highly structured environment like a Speed Networking event (where you are often provided with a list of attendees and their contact info.) Regardless of the setting, everyone should understand the etiquette of the business card exchange.

The first rule of thumb is that you should never ask for a business card as soon as you meet someone. Instead, wait until you have had a meaningful conversation. Need a reason to ask for his or her card? Think of a way you can offer to help your new acquaintance and request the person's contact information. When you receive the card, look at it and make some sort of positive comment about the card. It shows a genuine interest. At this point, your new contact will likely ask you for your card in return. You may want to hand out two or three cards at a time: one for the person you meet, and extras for him or her to hand out to referrals. (Offering to do the same would certainly be the polite thing to do in this case.)

A firm, warm handshake upon meeting a new contact is the ultimate person-to-person exchange, so don't overlook etiquette and common courtesy. Remember to make eye contact, smile and connect, thumb joint to thumb joint. Grasping at the fingertips just doesn't do! The handshake should always be a focused, meaningful moment of connection.

Fueling the Conversation with Storytelling Skills

If you have more than a minute to make an impression, you can expand on your Elevator Pitch in networking situations by telling stories. A well-crafted story can add color and clarity to your conversation while underscoring your background, qualifications and skills. Furthermore, by holding an audience's attention, storytellers succeed at networking by inspiring, persuading and ultimately connecting with their new contacts on an emotional level.

Prolific author, instructor and leading proponent of using storytelling for personal and professional advancement, Katharine Hansen, PhD, shares this valuable advice in her book *Tell Me About Yourself: Storytelling that Propels Careers:*

> *"Obviously, you don't want your expanded story to sound memorized. But you are, after all, talking about yourself, so the material is not hard to remember. It helps to write it out first—outline form is fine; then read it over a few times, and practice saying it without reading or memorizing it. Practice it in front of friends and members of your network, too. It's not a big deal if you forget a detail as long as you remember the main points.*
>
> *Remember that the point of composing such stories is not for them to sound exactly the way they are written. But writing them will help imprint them on your brain so you can tell them with the natural ease of a storyteller."*

A well-told story makes an impression on our memory and is, therefore, a great way to connect with new contacts. A few years ago, at a Speed Networking function, we hosted a woman who was a writer. She seemed different from the others in attendance; she was casual and friendly. While her fellow networkers were pitching products and services, she told a story…the same story to everyone she met that evening.

The story centered around a writing contest she entered when she was a little girl of seven years old. She explained the contest, her winning entry, the award ceremony, and the prize she won on that special day, so many years earlier.

The woman told me she would never forget hearing her name announced, walking proudly up to the podium to receive the grand prize. The principal of her grade school stretched out his hand; she shook it proudly. He told her that she was a great writer and to never stop. And then he gave her a package that she opened to reveal a dozen yellow pencils, engraved with her name. She told me how much she treasured the pencils as well as the pep talk he gave her. Then she reached into her purse and pulled out a brand new pack of yellow pencils. She handed me one; it had her name and her URL printed on the pencil. She told me very quickly about her business, which provides professional writing services, and asked me to visit her website to see her portfolio.

To this day, it was the best use of storytelling I have ever heard. It was unexpected, folksy and memorable. It was well-aligned with her past and her present situation. And it was absolutely impossible for me NOT to visit her website as soon as I got home from the event.

Part III

CONQUER

Chapter 10

YOU'VE CONNECTED. NOW CONQUER!

It was character that got us out of bed, commitment that moved us into action, and discipline that enabled us to follow through.

~ Zig Ziglar

So, you've perfected your Elevator Pitch, told some great stories, attended a few Speed Networking events. Great care and consideration have gone into establishing your newer and more complete network of contacts. You met many interesting people. And you would really like to help some of them with a reference or referral.

There's that nice dentist who specializes in pediatric care (your four-year-old niece is ready for her first teeth cleaning)...the bright student entering the work force (isn't your neighbor looking for a new associate?)...the experienced marketing consultant (your website is stagnant and virtually visitor-free)...that life coach with an inspirational attitude (your associate was just asking for a recommendation for one!).

Now you need to utilize the tools at your disposal to follow up and stay connected.

We always remind our Speed Networkers that their attendance at our events is not the end result or accomplishment of their efforts; it is just the beginning of a long-term relationship with others. Whether you have a slew of newly collected business cards or you received a list with contact information, you must act immediately to establish an ongoing rapport with the folks you just met.

Nurturing New Connections

When you return from a networking event, your mind may be bursting with fresh thoughts and ideas. Who stood out as someone you might be able to help? And how did they want you to contact them? Did someone ask for more information on your business or service? Did you suggest a follow-up lunch or phone call? Quick, jot it down!

Get to work nurturing your new connections:

1. **ENTER CONTACT INFO INTO A CONTACT MANAGEMENT SYSTEM:** Access an up-to-the-minute compilation of the best contact management systems for your needs. See Chapter 14 for details on Networking Karma's Tech Guide, exclusively for my readers.

2. **CONNECT WITH NEW CONTACTS ON LINKEDIN:** Send a quick invitation to connect but PLEASE take a moment to customize the standard, prepopulated

LinkedIn invitation. (We'll talk about this later in more detail.)

3. **FOLLOW YOUR NEW CONTACTS ON TWITTER:** Also, check out any blogs that your new contacts may have. And feel free to comment positively on one of their posts. What a great way to reinforce your first meeting.

4. **SEND A FOLLOW-UP EMAIL:** Don't wait more than forty-eight hours. Chances are you won't get around to it, and even if you do, the recipient may not remember you. Send an email to everyone with whom you exchanged cards. Remember, it doesn't matter if they can "help" you to achieve your goals; it's all about Karma. Gather the maximum amount of information on this new contact and think about how you can best continue the conversation.

5. **RELAY AN INTRODUCTION:** Find one person at each event and introduce him/her to someone else you think he or she should know. Where those two people take the relationship is up to them, but you will always be remembered as the person who made the introduction.

6. **GIVE THEM A CALL:** Today most business people tend to send out an email. They believe it is less intrusive and not as pushy, but it is also the least effective.

Steal These Email Messages!

Here's a go-to cheat sheet for your networking follow-up email needs. To nurture your new contacts, you need to make the information in your follow-up relevant. Think about sending along something related to your initial conversation. The following simple, concise email notes can be great tools for keeping new relationships going. Take a look!

Follow Up with a Related Article

Send your new contact an interesting news article related to your initial conversation.

> Dear Liz,
>
> It was great meeting you at the Speed Networking event last night. Enclosed is the article I mentioned to you, about the *Changing Role of the Real Estate Broker.* It hope you find it interesting—let me know what you think.
>
> Best,
> Sue Lerner

Follow Up with Feedback

Whether it is solicited or not, visit your new contacts' website and pay them a compliment, ask them a question, or comment on something interesting about the content or images.

> Dear Jordan,
>
> It was great meeting you at the Speed Networking event last night. You asked me to take a look at your website and provide feedback. Well, I think it is awesome. In fact, I believe it's award-worthy. I'm attaching the link to the 2015 Web wow Awards…I hope you'll enter for a chance to win as Best Website

in your field. Good luck and let me know the outcome. I'm rooting for you!!

Best,
Lisa Greening

Send an Invitation to a Can't-Miss Event They'll Appreciate

It's always good to get some insight into the personal interests of a new contact. Your email can build upon your initial conversation using a light, low-pressure approach.

Dear Steve,

It was nice meeting you last night at the Speed Networking event. I enjoyed learning about your business AND your personal interest in cinema. I am attaching an invitation to a screening of the upcoming film, *Yoda and The Monkey's Uncle*. Please enjoy it and get back to me with your review of the film!

Best,
Mike West

Make a Mutually Beneficial Connection or Referral

The key to networking is doing for others, and nothing is more thoughtful than providing a new contact with an opportunity to save time or money.

Dear Donna,

It was great meeting you last night at the Speed Networking event. During our brief exchange you mentioned your rising printing costs. For over ten years I have been working with a very reliable and affordable local printing company called ZapPrint. My contact there is Jamie. You can reach her at jsmith@zap.com. If you decide to call her, please let her know you are a friend of mine.

Good luck!
Jason

(…and don't forget to send an email to Jamie, letting her know that you passed on her name and number.)

Phone Call Follow-Up

Phone calls. They can't be edited. They can't be deleted. Maybe that's why so many of us prefer to send emails these days. Even so, hearing a voice on the other end of the phone is the next best thing to a face-to-face meeting. Phone calls can help to ratchet-up your relationship.

To-Dos

Keep your follow-up phone calls on track.

1. **DO YOUR HOMEWORK:** Before you place your call, Google your new contact and explore their website, read their LinkedIn profile or any other press they've received. Knowledge is power. You'll be in a better position to help your new contact if you understand what he/she does. Remember, Karma….

2. **BE IN A QUIET PLACE:** You might be a great multitasker, but making a call while you're driving in the

convertible with wind blowing through the receiver, or while on the sidelines during your child's soccer match (all the while hoping the game stays scoreless to avoid the inevitable cheers), is not the way to show someone you're interested in connecting with them. It is also a huge insult to waste someone's time by suggesting they "hang on" while you find a quieter place to talk.

3. **JOT DOWN A FEW NOTES:** No need to script your entire conversation, but jot down the main topics you'd like to discuss during the call.

4. **BE PREPARED FOR VOICEMAIL:** Organize your thoughts and speak clearly, slowly and concisely "after the beep..." Nothing is more pathetic than a flubbed voicemail message. And don't forget to leave your return phone number!

Follow-up to a Follow-up

According to a 2010 study from Yap, Inc., Americans receive seventy billion voicemail messages annually. That's a lot of calls to return! Still, if a week goes by without a reply to your initial contact, don't give up; try again. Be pleasantly persistent. Send a brief message, either by voice or email. It can be as simple as this:

> Hello, [contact's name], this is [your name]. I sent you a message/called last week and wanted to make one more attempt to reach you since you're probably incredibly busy. I know how crowded my voicemail gets every day! [Mention the reason for your original call.] Thanks and I look forward to your reply.

A Note About a Note

One of the best investments you can make is on personalized note cards. Whether you need to send a thank you, a birthday wish, a congratulatory message or even a follow-up to an interview, nothing shows sincerity and appreciation like a handwritten note, delivered by post.

Everyone wants to be remembered in a positive light. It is the key to standing out and making a lasting impression. And a handwritten note will do just that. So sit down with a small stack of your note cards every few days and quietly reflect on the recent past. Who do you need to thank, recognize or remember? Quickly jot down a few heart-felt words and drop your notes in the mail. Never wait until you NEED something to start this practice. Remember, Karma. Showing thoughtfulness and concern for others without expecting something in return often leads to great things down the road. What goes around comes around.

A Memento Makes You Memorable

Don't you just love receiving something unexpected through the mail? So will your new contacts!

A few years ago, I started working with a great promotional products company. They sell thousands of premiums and incentives that can be customized with a logo, url or phone number. One of the items they sell is a very inexpensive, bendable desk trinket. It looks like a little human figure with a clock in the middle. I ordered several hundred and had them branded with my logo and phone number.

Now, whenever I make a new acquaintance through business networking channels, I drop one of my little clocks in the mail with a note that says, "Thanks for your time."

Feel free to steal this idea or develop a clever gift that you can send and be remembered.

Chapter 11
LEVERAGING SOCIAL MEDIA

Social media is called social media for a reason.
It lends itself to sharing rather than horn-tooting.
~ Margaret Atwood

Facebook

In 2004, Facebook first emerged as a Harvard University-based social networking experiment. In a few short years, it forever changed our way of connecting with others and grew in a way we never could have imagined. At the beginning of 2014, Facebook had over 1.2 billion users.

Clearly, lots of people love Facebook. After all, Facebook makes it possible to stay in touch with friends and family, reconnect with those we've lost contact with and connect "virtually" with those who have common interests, ideas, issues and beliefs.

However, there are others who aren't so pleased with Facebook's influence on today's society. Many complain that Facebook and other social media outlets have led to mass anti-social behavior, especially among the younger generation. The lost art of conversation has given way to a more impersonal means of communication.

Another complaint: Facebook posts can be misconstrued. Feelings of isolation and exclusion are commonly experienced by active Facebook users. And of course, numerous articles have been written about the home-wrecking, divorce and infidelity that has occurred as a result of encounters with old flames on Facebook.

But whatever your opinion, you simply cannot dismiss Facebook as the most revolutionary development in human interaction since 1877, when the Bell Telephone Company brought telephones to the masses.

Using Facebook to Support Your Networking Efforts

With Facebook's limitless opportunities for networking come many more possibilities for missteps, faux pas and blunders. The boundaries between what is acceptable to share and what should be kept private are blurring, and networking rules are being rewritten constantly.

With this in mind it is no wonder that people are concerned with enlarging their circle to include—or "friend"—professional associates and potential business connections.

Sure, office etiquette has changed over the years. We are no longer shy about sharing personal stories, photos and plans with our office mates. But posting every comment, thought, outing and celebration for colleagues to see can unintentionally sabotage our attempts to build our personal brand. Just think of all the politicians, actors, celebrities and regular folks who had established themselves as mature, responsible and reliable, only to find themselves in hot water due to their social media networking activities.

Even if you are cautious with your status updates, posts and comments, your friends and family may post words or images to Facebook that could detract from the personal brand you worked so hard to develop and maintain.

For example, your college roommate could post an embarrassing shot of you at a toga party…your cousin might reminisce about your big-boy bed-wetting issues…your mom may nag you online, making you appear infantile.

These Facebook activities, while out of your control, are theoretically free for the world to see. Even with privacy settings in place, information about you can be shared via screen shots, and ultimately anything pumped through Facebook is hosted in "the cloud" and accessible to anyone intent on finding it. That's why my personal account is my link to close friends and family only.

Do I sound paranoid? Perhaps! That's why, in addition to my personal account, I have business pages set up on Facebook. There, I like to connect with new acquaintances, business prospects and professional colleagues and turn them into true fans of my businesses. I do not advise EVER soliciting business on Facebook; it's a smart place to share valuable information, news, tips and ideas. Hard selling, however, is a sure fire way to lose friends and fans, alike.

Another way to network on Facebook is to create a group. Whether it's established for alumni holiday party attendees, a book club or PhD candidates, the information shared in these groups helps facilitate plans, projects and discussions with others who share your interest.

"Friends" Enhance Your Life

In an earlier chapter I explained that the relationships you make and nurture help you increase your productivity, enhance your career and enrich your life in many ways.

Facebook allows you to nurture your existing relationships and start new ones, too. I have had life-enriching experiences thanks to personal Facebook connections.

I frequently call on my Facebook "friends" to provide me with advice, introductions and recommendations. My friends have turned me on to great philanthropic opportunities. I know people who have found everything from roommates to jobs through their Facebook friends. I even have a friend who found a buyer for his home via Facebook.

As you already know, not everything you want to accomplish in your life is within your power to complete alone, no matter how self-sufficient you are. Knowledge is power, and quite often it is your personal network that holds the knowledge you need to help you succeed. Isn't that reason enough to foray into Facebook?

To-Dos

Here are some ideas to consider for maximizing your personal networking success on Facebook.

1. **KEEP INVITES EXCLUSIVE:** If you've met people through a networking event or business function, there's really no need to invite them onto your personal Facebook page. It's much more appropriate for you to send them a LinkedIn invitation.

2. **ADJUST PRIVACY SETTINGS:** There's no reason to make your private information publicly available. The only people who should see what you post are your accepted friends and family.

3. **COMPLETE YOUR PROFILE:** The more information you provide, the easier it is to find your friends, classmates and family. Be cautious; keep your street address and other granular details of your life private.

4. **SPLIT CONTACTS INTO LISTS:** You may not want your neighbors and tennis pals to view the same information as your dearest friends and family. Facebook allows you to slice and dice your contacts and manage the information flow to each list.

5. **USE COMMON SENSE:** Everything in moderation. If you are posting religious, political, emotional or hostile content every day, you may alienate those who are reading.

6. **STAY ABREAST OF DEVELOPMENTS:** Facebook is always changing; new services and apps are constantly being introduced to its users. And more and better functionality is being launched every day. Maximize your Facebook experience by staying on the cutting edge.

7. **ENGAGE YOUR NETWORK:** To make the most of your time on Facebook, keep the conversation going. Respond to your friends, comment on posts, "Like" comments and pictures, and provide suggestions when requested. When you post your status, keep your voice interactive. Rather than making a statement, ask a question, share a story or make an observation.

8. **BE SINCERE:** Never use your personal Facebook page as a marketing platform. "Selling" your friends is a turn-off. Instead, make offers to help your friends, connect people to opportunities, and be genuine in all of your communications. When you do have a personal or career success, feel free to post it to your friends and family. Just don't make it a daily occurrence. (That's what LinkedIn is for!)

LinkedIn

As mentioned (but worth repeating), when following up to the success of a networking event, it is imperative that you reach out and continue to build rapport with your new connections immediately. One of the very first steps you can take is to extend invitations to your new contacts, asking them to join your LinkedIn network. It is a great way to keep them up-to-date on your activities, and vice-versa.

LinkedIn has revolutionized the professional networking world. Not only has it allowed tens of millions of people around the globe to share their experience, knowledge and work status with their colleagues and contacts, it has given us a unique ability to reach past our immediate circle, connect with like-minded professionals and follow those in whom we take an interest. LinkedIn also allows you to extend your reach—via your connection's connections—giving you the potential to meet anyone in the world (as long as they, too, are a LinkedIn user). Of course, LinkedIn is fast becoming one of the greatest sources for job leads and, simultaneously becoming the ultimate sandbox for recruiters to play in.

As a LinkedIn member, your profile is akin to your personal billboard and as such, it needs to grab the attention of all who see it; using all the right words and images is crucial.

Optimize Your LinkedIn Profile

LinkedIn is the world's largest professional network with over three hundred million members. Your LinkedIn profile offers a unique opportunity to brand yourself as a polished professional and yet so very few professionals leverage this amazing tool. Think of it this way: if your resume is your career history, your LinkedIn profile is your career future! This is where you want to DELIVER VALUE and SELL YOURSELF! You wouldn't go to a networking event half-dressed, so why is your LinkedIn profile not complete?

Donna Serdula, social media advisor, speaker and author of the book, *Professional Secrets to a POWERFUL LinkedIn Profile,* shares these ten quick tips to get your LinkedIn profile shining!

1. **START AT THE BOTTOM:** The easy sections are at the bottom of your profile…so start at the end and work your way up. By starting at the bottom, you are less likely to get intimidated and quit.

2. **DETERMINE YOUR GOAL:** What are you hoping to achieve by having a LinkedIn profile? Who is your desired reader? What does your audience want to learn about you? Write your profile with your goal and reader in mind.

3. **INCLUDE YOUR CONTACT INFO:** If you don't include your contact information, how will opportunity know which door to knock on?

4. **GET THREE RECOMMENDATIONS:** Three recommendations bring your profile fifteen percent closer to one hundred percent complete. Reach out and request recommendations from customers and people in high places!

   LinkedIn recommendations are a great way to let others promote YOU!

5. **LIST THREE PAST JOB EXPERIENCES:** You need three experiences to achieve a one hundred percent complete profile. Provide a summary on the company, explain your responsibilities and tell a brief story of a success. Profiles that are one hundred percent complete are forty times more likely to show up in LinkedIn search results.

6. **WRITE YOUR SUMMARY IN THE FIRST PERSON:** Don't copy and paste your resume into your Summary! Write in the first person and talk about your strengths. Describe a key achievement. Talk about your guiding career philosophy.

7. **CREATE A POWERFUL HEADLINE:** Create a compelling headline by summarizing what you do in a short sentence. Start the sentence with something like "Helping Businesses achieve...."

8. **SAY CHEESE:** Get a professional photographer to snap your picture. You've spent time making sure your

profile is polished and professional; now make sure you look good!

9. **CLAIM YOUR PUBLIC PROFILE URL:** Use your name or some variant of your name to make a memorable LinkedIn Public Profile URL that you can market on your email signature and other places.

10. **KEEP IT REAL AND BE YOURSELF:** Stay away from "resume speak" and corporate jargon. Write conversationally and speak from your heart. Don't be shy; tell the world your value and strengths!

Making First Impressions Count on LinkedIn

Let's circle back around to that idea of the all-important first impression. As in Speed Networking, following up on your networking relationships through LinkedIn requires that you put your best foot forward and align yourself, your profile, and all of your LinkedIn activity with your brand standards.

But keep in mind that, although Speed Networking is about maximizing the number of contacts you make, it is never smart to come across as someone simply trying to rack up a large number of contacts. You want your prospective new LinkedIn connection to feel as if he is taking the first step to building a lasting mutual relationship.

So give some thought to the first "written" impression you will make upon your new contact.

How do you feel when you receive a LinkedIn invitation with the boilerplate intro rather than a customized one? Don't you wish someone had taken a moment or two to add a bit of warmth, some context and some encouraging words about how the connection might benefit YOU? Those cookie cutter LinkedIn invitations do nothing for first impressions. They make the sender come across as self-serving and lazy.

In a real world conversation, you wouldn't blurt out, "I'd like to add you to my network of contacts," would you? Of course not! You would start off with a polite greeting (Hello, Hi, Dear Joe,) and then go on to very concisely introduce yourself and explain why you are reaching out to the person ("We met at last night's Speed Networking event").

Dale Carnegie once said, "There is only one way…to get anybody to do anything. And that is by making the other person want to do it." Keeping this quote in mind, you can certainly get your prospective new contact to join you on LinkedIn by finding a way to make them WANT to do it. How? It's fine to ask them directly to join your network but why not add, "Let's see how we can help each other succeed" or "I've been giving some thought to how I might be able to help you." Who wouldn't want to respond to the friendly offer of assistance? Finally, close your invitation with a polite statement, like "It was a pleasure meeting you" or "I look forward to keeping up with you on LinkedIn."

The above advice also holds true for new contacts you make in any environment. You will be remembered and respected for the personal touches you add to the standard boilerplate messaging.

Six Degrees of Separation: Give It a Try on LinkedIn

By now, you've probably heard the principles of Six Degrees of Separation. Some researchers have dispelled the theory while others have been able to support it. Either way, it is an idea that we are all connected by no more than six links between us.

Using your connections you can actually map out your route and connect with virtually any other person on LinkedIn through your primary (first) or secondary (second) connections. Give it a try!

A Success Story

I "met" Ed through a Group on LinkedIn. We both participated in so many common "threads" and found, through our comments, that we were like-minded. After a few friendly conversations, we connected. We've never met face-to-face. He lives in Manchester, UK.

I am also connected to a former colleague named Laurel. She read my status update and noticed that I had a new connection from Manchester. She contacted me right away to tell me that her brother, Bruce, was planning to relocate to Manchester. She noticed that my new contact, Ed, worked for a technology company there. Since Bruce was searching for a position as a computer engineer, she thought that Ed and Bruce should be introduced and asked if I would make the introduction. I did so through LinkedIn.

Coincidentally, Ed's college roommate Tom was investing in a technology start-up firm. Ed was kind enough to introduce Bruce to Tom via LinkedIn. One thing led to another and now Bruce is working as a consultant for Tom's new venture in the Manchester area.

Success in LESS than six degrees! That's how LinkedIn's huge contribution to the business community is making the world smaller and more accessible to all of us.

Thought Leadership and LinkedIn

According to several sources, the term "Thought Leader" was first coined in 1994 by Joel Kurtzman, Editor-in-Chief of what was then a Booz, Allen & Hamilton magazine, *Strategy & Business.* Seventeen years later, the term has become somewhat of a catch phrase (some would argue it's one of the most overused phrases in the business lexicon) and everyone is clamoring to become a "Thought Leader" if they aren't a self-proclaimed one already!

What is a Thought Leader, really? And how can being a Thought Leader help you in your Speed Networking and beyond? Let's explore.

If you want to be recognized by your network as someone who is highly knowledgeable in your working "space"—someone who truly understands the problems (and solutions) for their customers, and someone who has a full perspective of the competitive landscape of their business—then you need to become a Thought Leader. Once your network recognizes your expertise, they will keep you in the forefront of their minds and think of you when your expertise is needed. But that isn't the only benefit. As a Thought Leader, you will also attract new contacts and this will serve to grow your network exponentially.

One great way to raise your TLQ (Thought Leadership Quotient) is to create and publish long form posts on LinkedIn. These blog-like articles allow you to share your professional insight with a network of like-minded professionals who are hungry for your expert content. Besides sparking conversations and building your reputation, these posts can sometimes go viral, thus spreading your name to many outside your network.

Build Relationships Through LinkedIn Groups

As a LinkedIn member, you can join up to fifty groups. The more groups you join, the more chances you have to elevate your profile with the population by which you want to be recognized. By being active in meaningful discussions, you can position yourself as an expert within the group. Once you become an active participant, the others in the group may see some synergy, reach out and request that you join their network (or vice versa). As I mentioned on the previous page, this is how many meaningful business relationships get their start these days.

It is easy to find groups that match your interest. Simply use the search box in the top right-hand corner and type in the keywords that fit your expertise or interest. Some groups have a screening process that excludes those who do not have relevant work experience.

Another option is to start a group. As the manager of your group, you can control the content of the discussions and your audience will recognize you as a leader in your field. Perhaps you are a doctor looking to connect with others in the medical field. Or maybe you are involved in journalism and hoping to develop a large network of others. By creating a group, LinkedIn will allow you to reach beyond your own personal network and start discussions, share news and even post jobs. But there's more! You can then form subgroups, based on location, and create meeting opportunities where your fellow, faceless online connections can further their relationships by sitting down, face-to-face, and really maximizing engagement.

Form a Group and Make Things Happen

As a staffing strategist, it is vital that I stay abreast of the latest HR developments across every industry that I serve. This sentiment was the driving force in my decision to create a LinkedIn Group of local HR professionals. Apparently, I was not the only one looking to connect to others in this niche.

Dozens turned into hundreds, and before long there were over one thousand members in my Human Resources NJ LinkedIn Group. Not only do we use LinkedIn to share, debate and support each other, we also connect face-to-face. I have organized several live events featuring expert speakers from various HR disciplines and have conducted Speed Networking events. As you might imagine, the success of these events has generated many new personal and professional contacts for everyone involved. Perhaps best of all, it has been very rewarding for me to be a positive force in my industry.

Providing Feedback on LinkedIn

Whether you are answering a question or commenting on a post, it is very important that you provide factual responses, NOT sales pitches. Networking is about Karma. It's about giving and then getting back what you give. Provide unbiased knowledge, help and advice. Do this without trying to sell yourself and something good will come back to you.

One other comment about providing feedback on LinkedIn: never try to make yourself look intelligent or well-connected at the expense of another person in your peer group. It is OK to disagree with someone's feedback, but do so in a collegial way. A know-it-all looks like a bully when belittling other peoples' comments. Remember, hundreds if not thousands of like-minded pros are reading your posts. Many folks who try to flex their intellect on LinkedIn end up falling flat on their face.

Twitter

"What's happening?'

Those two little words call out to you on Twitter's home page. You draw a blank. Baffled by what to write and how to engage others, you decide to take the Twitter plunge at some later date.

Sound familiar? All too often people bypass Twitter because of uncertainty; after all, Twitter's interface and character limitations are certainly not intuitive. But this shouldn't be an excuse to squander a great platform for building your network, reinforcing your personal brand, and shaping the message you want to convey to others.

Through our own networking efforts, we established a great working relationship with Steve Goldner, (aka Social Steve) Chief Engagement Officer, Social Steve Consulting. We asked him, "What should the strategy be for using Twitter for people looking to build their network?" His answer:

> *"The funny thing is that most start with that question and try to build a Twitter strategy...that is the wrong place to begin. Yes, Twitter can be a most useful tool, but if it is the starting point, failure is certain."*

To-Dos

Here is Social Steve's advice on implementing Twitter for networking success.

1. **ASK YOURSELF: "HOW DO I WANT TO BE PERCEIVED?"** Social Steve says, "I started using Twitter about five years ago and even before I dipped my toe in the water, I asked myself, 'What is my brand?' Before YOU start communicating anywhere, make sure you know exactly how YOU want to be perceived. I'll use myself as an example. I want to be viewed as a down-to-earth marketing and social media Thought Leader. Thus, my Twitter name is SocialSteve."

2. **CREATE CONTENT THAT ALIGNS WITH YOUR BRAND:** "Labels do not go far, unless they are supported with awesome content. Content that reinforces your brand. Thus, my tweeting covers marketing,

social media, and light topics such as family outings and music. The marketing and social media tweets aim to promote my position as a Thought Leader in the space. The tweets about family outings and seeing and listening to music I love add some of my own personality behind my brand. I think everyone needs to come across as down-to-earth, real, and personable in the Twitter space."

3. **DEVELOP COMPELLING QUIPS IN 140 CHARACTERS OR LESS:** "Twitter is poor for content production. It is great for headlines and one-liners, but not the best communication tool for rich content that truly establishes the brand position you seek as an individual."

4. **USE TWITTER TO POINT TO YOUR BEST CONTENT:** "If you want to come across as an expert in a particular area and someone who people want to connect with, you need to use other platforms such as blogs and LinkedIn to post the content that reinforces the perception you seek to capture."

5. **CURATE THE CONTENT OF OTHERS:** "A word of caution—do not just tweet and post YOUR content. Curate content. Look for great examples of others' content that supports your position. If you want to be the reference point for your area of expertise, you need a good balance of your own media and curated media. As you deliver value and establish this balance, you will capture earned media."

6. **EXPRESS YOUR INDIVIDUALITY:** "Don't forget to sprinkle some funny anecdotes or personal experiences to put some personality behind your Twitter presence."

7. **SET REALISTIC OBJECTIVES:** "I don't care about how many followers I have. I care about getting the right people to follow me. I have built a slow, modest following over the years. I do not worry about the numbers, but I remain committed to delivering best practice and leading advice to my audience. As a result, I continue to see a small growth every week."

Social media has changed the way we connect. It allows us to provide value, build awareness, nurture relationships and establish our relevance in the areas that interest us. The challenge is to decide on which platforms to be active. In addition to those mentioned above, there are also Google+, YouTube, Pinterest, Instagram and a host of others.

It's virtually impossible to have the time to be relevant everywhere, and understanding all of the nuances of the particular platforms requires deep analysis. Certainly, there's a plethora of advice and insight on the different social networks. As you formulate your social media networking strategy, I suggest first doing some research to determine the online destinations where your ideal contacts might "hang out."

Chapter 12
MENTORING

"The mediocre leader tells.
The good leader explains.
The superior leader demonstrates.
The great leader inspires."
~ Gary Patton

No discussion of networking would be complete without the mention of mentoring. After all, many believe that networking is nothing more than an informal matrix of mentors. Like networking itself, mentoring is about building relationships, helping others, and sharing information and ideas. Whether your mentor/mentee relationship is formal or informal, there is much to give and to gain from your participation.

Informal Mentoring

Robin had Batman. Alexander the Great had Aristotle. Oliver Stone had Martin Scorsese and even rapper Eminem has Dr. Dre. These successful relationships were not developed through structured clubs, groups or associations. They most likely started with a handshake and this probing question...

"How did you do that?"

A nugget of learning most likely turned into a follow-up discussion. A chat on the telephone (or by bat phone or carrier pigeon) led to another get-together. And that meeting developed into a trusted partnership of sharing and guidance.

Whether you are in a position to advise others or accept the counsel of someone more experienced than you, you must be in the right frame of mind and be open to taking on the responsibilities inherent to the roles that make mentoring work.

As a mentor in an informal situation, you need to be able to share stories of success as well as failure. Your role is to offer constructive feedback and empower your mentee to grow as a result of your connection. On the other hand, as a mentee in an informal situation, you MUST take responsibility for communicating and following up with your mentor, to keep him or her in the loop with your personal and professional progress. It is also vital that you have realistic expectations; this is not a "what can you do for me?" scenario. If you show appreciation and value the advice you receive, the relationship can flourish and ultimately you may reap rewards from it.

What rewards, you ask? Well, like networking, mentoring is all about Karma. What goes around comes around. The mentor gives of his or her time and knowledge and gets much in return: an opportunity to learn from the protégé, to enhance leadership skills and also, in some cases, the chance to leave a legacy of knowledge or skills.

On the other hand, the mentee or protégé gets to ramp up personal development, receives fresh insight, builds skills, meets new people and, most importantly, gains a supportive and trusted sounding board.

Is mentoring simply a label for what happens naturally among like-minded, motivated people who know, respect and trust each other? Could be! If you're looking for an informal mentor, go ahead and find an open, experienced and thoughtful brain to pick. Start a conversation. Bounce some ideas around. Over time, your mentor/mentee relationship may be born.

Formal Mentoring

Today, thanks to Internet search tools, you can connect with mentoring opportunities quickly and easily. Whether you are looking for a mentor or want to be one (to a child, a college student, someone in the special-needs population, a young colleague or a person in transition), you can sign on with a structured mentoring program that fosters quality mentoring relationships. There are literally thousands of well-established mentoring programs in every state and in virtually every country.

These programs often provide training, placement and even convenient meeting locations. In addition, you may be furnished with a "toolkit" for successful relationship development. From planning schedules to contracts—from checklists to worksheets—great mentoring organizations equip their volunteers with the materials they need for goal-setting and collecting feedback, all to move the participants forward in their mutual efforts.

Formal mentoring programs differ from informal mentoring programs in a number of ways. First and foremost, a screening process is usually in place to determine the right formal mentoring "match." Credentials of both parties may be checked for legitimacy.

Once a match is made, a mutual "contract" is signed. This document outlines the goals of both parties, best practices for success, and other vital guidelines. An organizational structure is agreed upon, which specifies how, when and where the mentorship meetings will occur. A formal timeline is also established; depending on the program and the participants' goals, the mentorship arrangement will either have a predetermined end date or meetings will be on-going. There will also be details on how to dissolve the relationship if it is not a successful one.

A good mentoring program has just as many benefits—concrete and intangible—for the mentor as the mentee. As a formal mentor, you'll build your leadership skills and gain recognition from friends, colleagues and, quite possibly, the management of your organization. On a personal level, you may enhance your self-awareness and sense of accomplishment. You may also have a chance to build your network through the mentoring program with which you associate. Perhaps best of all, you will enhance the future of your mentee through your good work. And, who knows, Karma may repay you with other, unknown opportunities.

On the other hand, as a mentee in a formal program, you will certainly learn about your personal strengths, weaknesses and areas for development; all of this information will allow you, the mentee, to ultimately take more control of your future. If applicable, you'll develop professional skills and a broader knowledge base, and get a fresher perspective on your professional and personal journey. Mentees often benefit by getting access to their mentor's personal network. Ultimately, the support of your mentor will allow you to work more efficiently and effectively toward your goals.

The career and financial benefits to a formal corporate program have been studied and the results are staggering. Sun

Microsystems tracked the careers of about one thousand team members involved in mentoring over a five-year period. Here's what they learned:

- Mentors and mentees were more than twenty percent more likely to have received a raise than those who did not mentor
- Twenty-five percent of mentees got a raise
- Twenty-eight percent of mentors got a raise
- Mentees were promoted four times more often than those without mentors
- Mentors were six times more likely to receive promotions than their counterparts.

Beyond promoting personal growth and goal-setting, the professional benefits acquired from mentoring relationships have the potential to be dramatic.

To-Dos

A mentor's checklist for success.

1. **PROVIDE EXPERTISE:** Whether it is professional, academic or life skills, be sure you have the expertise needed for the mentee to succeed.

2. **BE APPROACHABLE:** Your genuine concern and openness will enable your mentee to gain the full benefit of all you have to offer.

3. **GUIDE BUT DON'T CONTROL:** Your role is to empower, not smother, your mentee.

4. **CHALLENGE NEGATIVE BELIEFS:** Facilitate improvement in all areas for your mentee by building confidence through positive thinking.

5. **PROVIDE CONSTRUCTIVE FEEDBACK:** First, listen. Then, be honest and direct but never judgmental in your critiques. Highlight strengths and recognize developmental needs.

6. **PREPARE FOR YOUR ROLE:** Commit to and take mentoring seriously. Be organized, take notes, set goals and summarize vital points of enlightenment along the way for your mentee.

Chapter 13

HOSTING A SPEED NETWORKING EVENT

When you do the common things in life in an uncommon way, you will command the attention of the world.

~ George Washington Carver

Lots of people ask me, "How on earth did a successful staffing professional get involved in Speed Networking?" It's a great question that I'm happy to answer. Here's how it all started.

> As an agency recruiter, my number-one priority has always been to build and sustain a broad, diverse talent pool. But there is one major challenge to achieving this. As mentioned earlier in the book, I am an introvert and the thought of networking has always made my skin crawl.

One day, while I was scanning EventBrite for upcoming networking opportunities, I saw an ad for a local Speed Networking event. I figured I'd give it a try. After all, I knew Speed Dating worked—a friend met her husband this way—and it looked like fun. I assumed that the two followed similar formats.

Within minutes of my arrival at the function, I felt the stress evaporate from my body. A sense of renewed confidence and competence filled the air. The structure of the event removed virtually every networking stumbling block I had ever encountered. No awkward introductions, no dreadfully long sales pitches, no painful rejections or long good-byes. I was hooked.

As I watched the others in the room move from seat to seat, meeting dozens of interesting, friendly professionals, I thought, "Wow, what a great way for people to connect." And that was my "Aha!" moment.

Speed Networking seemed like a natural fit with my recruiting business. After all, I already helped companies to grow by connecting them with talent. Why not help regular folks: job seekers or those returning to the work force or just those wanting to branch out? I was immediately inspired and intrigued. I wanted IN! I thought Speed Networking was the answer and I saw areas for improvement...many ways I could tweak the process, the venue and the atmosphere, to make Speed Networking even better.

As the buzz about my new business grew louder, a funny thing happened. Karma. Or, to be more precise, Networking Karma. As host of these events, I was helping people. And the positive vibes came back to me. I never realized that I would become the most visible person in the room. I became memorable. People knew my name. They told their friends about me. Word spread. Speed Networking was the key to Networking Karma!

To build my circle of influence, I didn't need to attend dozens of events, shake hundreds of hands or rattle off Elevator Pitches ad nauseam. I just needed to plan an event, create a memorable networking experience, and send my attendees home with a great story to tell.

My Speed Networking events have been a huge success. They are exciting, fast paced and unexpectedly fun. Speed Networking has allowed me to build my pool of passive job candidates. It has also helped me to establish my own personal and professional brand. Within my industry, I've become known as a creative, strategic and innovative recruiter and networker. I would like to think that I have been consistent and authentic in sustaining this brand promise.

If you want to make a splash in your "space," think about becoming a Speed Networking host. I haven't found a better, more fun or fulfilling way to engage new contacts and build my network.

It is important to note that as you foray into the Speed Networking event planning business, you may not necessarily have immediate financial profit or receive instant gratification in the form of referrals or business leads. Like networking itself, becoming a Speed Networking event host is a long-term proposition. However, there are limitless opportunities for you to reach your full potential.

To-Dos

Fool-Proof Tips for First-Time Speed Networking Hosts

Imagine if you were planning a large get-together at your home. The success of the evening would depend on how much advanced planning you did and special details you arranged for your guests. The same goes for networking event planning. The big picture has to be mapped out far in advance and the small details set you and your event apart from the rest.

1. **CREATE SPREADSHEETS AND DATABASES:** You'll need to track everything from expenditures to income, attendees to referrals. You'll also need to avoid redundancies in your guest list (for instance, you can't have six stock brokers in attendance!) Organization is key to running your networking business.

2. **MAKE A BUDGET:** The only way to manage your business intelligently is to keep a handle on the spending. This may seem obvious but it is the number one mistake of all failed start-ups.

3. **DEVELOP SPONSORSHIPS AND/OR PARTNERSHIPS:** Think strategically about connecting with like-minded individuals or companies to increase resources and build exposure to your networking events.

4. **CHOOSE YOUR SPACE WISELY:** Consider all sensory experiences when selecting a location for your event. Everything from the acoustics to the lighting to the temperature to the odors is important. Equally vital

is finding a catering team or proprietor with whom you work well.

5. **SWEAT THE DETAILS:** From the moment your guests enter the room, be sure they are put at ease. Use your best manners. Smile. Greet your guests at the door. Introduce people and do what you can to alleviate their worries. (Some event planners like to offer a cash bar or a complimentary cocktail.) Remember: People DO stress out about attending networking events. Reassure them that this will be fun and different.

6. **PROVIDE A TOOLBOX FOR SUCCESS:** Your guests are more apt to succeed at Speed Networking if they are given: water and/or mints, pads and pens to take notes, a canvas bag or small tote to collect business cards and other information. And perhaps most importantly, give clear direction! After all, one of the keys to a great Speed Networking experience is having an effective host who can monitor the flow of the event.

One final word on this subject: Never, ever, ever use your Speed Networking event as a platform to "sell" yourself or your business. This is a TOTAL turn off! My very first Speed Networking experience featured a host who spent a large chunk of time promoting his payroll business. To me, this tactic totally contradicted everything that networking stands for. As I said earlier, the most successful networkers are on a constant mission of "giving." Stealing valuable time from the attendees to self-promote flies in the face of this ideal.

Those who attend my Speednetworx™ events generally have no idea that I have another business.

So remember: You are the host. You are there to communicate, monitor and calmly direct the "flow" of attendees. Do your job right and word-of-mouth will propel your events forward.

Check out these resources for helping you to plan your events.

icebreakertags.com
A clever site that allows you to customize and generate intriguing, conversation-starting name tags.

networkingresearchgroup.com
Create customized apps for conferences to improve networking and enhance deal-making among attendees.

eventbrite.com
A free, easy to use event management tool to help you promote and sell your event, and track reservations online.

Chapter 14
WHAT'S NEXT?

"It comes from within. The discipline to dig deeper. The guts to be real. The passion to build your dream. The commitment to connect. The strength to defy your struggle. Everything is possible"
~ Gail Tolstoi-Miller

Congratulations! You've made it to the final pages of Networking Karma. You now have an abundance of insight, information and ideas that will help you to give and get the most out of every current and future relationship you develop. I truly believe that understanding the karmic nature of networking is the edge you need to succeed in business and in life. In fact, this core concept is the centerpiece of my business, career and networking coaching curriculum.

Hopefully, you're not too overwhelmed with all of the steps and tips provided in this book.

If you're not sure how to get where you want to be with your networking, keep reading! Whether you're inspired to attend your first Speed Networking event, encouraged to update your business cards, ready to create a LinkedIn profile, or excited to start reaching out to make introductions, it's time to roll up your sleeves and get to work.

First, take a moment to think about your networking objectives. What do you want to achieve? Remember that objectives need to be distinct, feasible and measurable. For example, maybe you are determined to join two industry related networking groups. Or create three social media accounts. These are great goals! Think about how much time you'll need to meet these objectives and what it's going to take to get there. Perhaps you'll need to pen your LinkedIn profile, or purchase new networking attire, or even revamp your business cards. Are you willing to set priorities, respect deadlines and accept that failure and setbacks are part of the journey? If so, you'll soon be celebrating your networking success!

You've come this far. Don't stop until you've taken in this last chapter. It's chock full of helpful, hands-on guides and resources that will be absolutely vital in turning your networking plans into relationship reality.

NETWORKING KARMA DOWNLOADS

In this section I'll introduce you to additional tools and activities to help you achieve Networking Karma. These can be found in their entirety on this book's web site: www.networkingkarmabook.com

Use the exclusive readers' code ***NKVAULT*** to unlock the following valuable resources online.

Networking Survival Guide

This useful resource of pre- and post-networking strategies will help you be more prepared, avoid the pitfalls and eliminate the stress and apprehension of networking events.

Networking Karma Action Planner

A valuable template that will make it easy to create distinct plans of action and meet your networking milestone.

Social Media Cheat Sheet

Twitter! LinkedIn! Facebook! If you're overwhelmed with where to start and what to say, this easy-to-read grid clarifies guidelines for creating and sharing content on several relevant platforms and prioritizes the steps to engage and grow your network.

Speed Networking Event Planning Checklist

Get step-by-step to-dos to help you plan your own Speed Networking event, where everyone will remember YOU! Plus, get my exclusive list of TOP Networking Event Myths and Mistakes.

College Student Networking Success Secrets

From finding the perfect roommate, to landing that first internship or REAL job, anything is possible when you have a strong network. Learn the secrets to shoring up connections for mutual success.

Networking Karma Tech Guide

From cutting-edge business card apps to hot new CMS platforms, this lineup of time-saving tools and services is geared toward networking success.

Exclusive LinkedIn Networking Karma Group

You will receive lifetime membership to our Networking Karma LinkedIn Group. This closely managed and monitored online meeting place connects you with fellow readers who could become future employers, friends or customers. Find us on LinkedIn and submit your request for membership. We will reach out to request the reader code ***NKVAULT***. This is the key to unlocking the power of Networking Karma with helpful Q&A, advice, tips and support.

If you find the above-mentioned downloads and the information in this book invaluable, tweet your favorite tips and ideas to your connections! Reference #networkingkarma as your source for inspiration. Thank you.

Get Inspired To Take the Next Step

Networking helps you foster relationships to further yourself and your contacts in every aspect of life. It is a vital skill that allows you to fulfill your true potential. When I discovered Speed Networking and integrated it into my relationship development efforts, I saw my dreams take shape and soon my goals were within reach. I sincerely hope this book brings you closer to achieving all that you want, too.

After all, everyone has what it takes to be a successful networker. All you need is a little preparation, practice and patience. And a little inspiration helps, too.

When will you finally be moved to take your networking to the next level? When will you follow your dreams, step out of your comfort zone, take control and be inspired to create the life that you want?

Are you still waiting for that "Aha!" moment?

I dug through my iTunes movie library to bring you the following motivational movies. As you rev up your engine and get ready to network at full throttle, take in one of these inspirational movies;

their messages will stay with you long after you reach the final scene, and help motivate you on your road to networking success.

Dead Poet's Society

A misfit English teacher takes a staid boy's prep school by storm as he uses his unconventional teaching approach to inspire his students' creativity and individuality.

Take-away: ***Carpe Diem: Seize the Day.*** Sometimes we get so caught up in what others expect of us that we forget ourselves in the process. This film beautifully reminds us to look at things differently, to question convention, and to make the most of every moment.

The Pursuit of Happyness

A true story of an out-of-work dad's relentless attempt to achieve all that he KNOWS he is worth.

Take-away: ***Never Give Up on Your Goals.*** An unforgettably uplifting story of success in the face of adversity and a testament to the strength of the human spirit.

Rocky

A lowly boxer from the streets of Philadelphia climbs to the top of the boxing world with nothing but muscle and the will to win.

Take-away: ***Go the Distance.*** This classic not only had a profound effect on the genre of sports films, it also leaves a lasting impression on virtually all who see it. Watch it again, and remember why you walked out of the theatre, ready to take on the world!

Field of Dreams

A farmer is compelled by voices to build a baseball diamond in his corn field. Although everyone thinks he's nuts, he does it. And the long-gone Chicago Black Sox come to play in his field of dreams.

Take-away: ***Believe in Your Dream.*** Do you have a "vision" for your future? This film reminds you that no one needs to understand your vision but you.

Pay It Forward

A young boy is given an assignment to come up with a plan to change the world. His idea: to do a good deed for three people and ask them, not to return the favor, but to "pay it forward" to three others in need.

Take-away: ***What Goes Around Comes Around.*** The ultimate Karmic tale...Do you believe that the obligation to help others can spread exponentially throughout the world, creating a social movement intended to make the world a better place? If so, start networking today!

I hope these works of inspiration ignite the words I shared at the beginning of this book: YOU possess the capacity to change your life through the relationships you develop. So connect with people. Learn their story. Help them if you can. Build your network and you'll find true joy, satisfaction and strength.

"We cannot build our own future without helping others to build theirs."

~ President Bill Clinton

EPILOGUE

In the midst of writing this book, I was stunned by a diagnosis of breast cancer. Once I recovered from the shock, I went into networking overdrive, connecting with medical professionals, other patients and survivors for mutual support. Though I kept my health a private matter from most for about a year, I chose not to be silent with generous fellow cancer patients and close friends, many of whom helped me to obtain the best information about treatments, holistic measures, insurance and more. I gave kindness, care and compassionate support in equal measure, made deep and meaningful connections, and saw the profound impact of Networking Karma.

In the previous pages I have tried to share with you how vital networking is for your business and your career. But above all else, it is crucial that you come away with the understanding that networking may actually help you save a life—maybe someone else's. Maybe even your own.

REFERENCES

Wolff, Hans-Georg and Klaus Moser. *Effects of Networking on Career Success: A Longitudinal Study*, Journal of Applied Psychology 94;1 (2009): 196–206.

Webster's Dictionary. www.miriam-webster.com/dictionary/karma.

Vandell, R.A.; Davis, R.A.; Clugston, H.A. *The Function of Mental Practice in the Acquisition of Motor Skills*. Journal of General Psychology, Vol 29, (1943): 243–250.

Frerker, Terry. *Speed Networking for Business Success*, Excellence In Business, last modified September 5, 2010, ***http://excellenceinbusiness.org/?s=speed+networking***.

Finkel, Eli J. and Paul W. Eastwick. *Speed-Dating*, Current Directions in Psychological Science 17; 3 (2008). ***http://people.tamu.edu/~eastwick/FinkelEastwick_CDir.pdf***

MacMillan Dictionary. ***www.macmillandictionary.com/buzzword/entries/speed-networking.html***.

Paton, Nic. *Speed Dating Giving Way to Speed Networking*, Management-Issues, last modified July 22, 2005, ***http://www.management-issues.com/2006/8/24/research/speed-dating-giving-way-to-speed-networking.asp.***

McGregor, Jena. *Speed Dating For Suits*, BusinessWeek, last modified September 11, 2006 ***http://www.businessweek.com/magazine/content/06_37/b4000088.htm.***

The Marriage Killer: One in Five American Divorces Now Involve Facebook. Gardner, David (December 1, 2010)." *Daily Mail* (London).

Wilson, Lyndsay. *Top 5 Reasons to Visualize*, last modified March 19, 2012, http://www.mymentaltoughness.com.

Frost, Robert. *The Road Not Taken and Other Poems* (New York: Henry Holt and Co., 1916).

Sunnafrank, M. *Journal of Social and Personal Relationships*, 21(3): 361–379.

Inventor of the Week: Archive. Massachusetts Institute of Technology, September, 2000. http://lemelson.mit.edu/resources/alexander-graham-bell

Bellezza, Silvia, Gilo, Francesca and Keinan, Anat. *The Red Sneakers Effect: Inferring Status and Competence from Signals of Nonconformity*, Journal of Consumer Research, 2014. ***http://www.hbs.edu/faculty/Publication%20Files/The%20Red%20Sneakers%20Effect%202014_4657b733-84f0-4ed6-a441-d401bbbac19d.pdf***

Jack, Rachael E., Caldara, Roberto and Philippe G. Schyns. *Internal Representations Reveal Cultural Diversity in Expectations of Facial Expressions of Emotion*, Journal of Experimental Psychology, 141(1).

Personal Care Activities. United States Department of Labor (2010), accessed April 3, 2012, http://www.bls.gov/tus/current/personal.htm.

Elevator Pitch Builder. Harvard Business Review (2007), accessed April 5, 2012, http://www.alumni.hbs.edu/careers/pitch/.

Brown, J. Mariah. *How Can Cultural Differences Affect Business Communications?* Demand Media, accessed May 12, 2012, http://smallbusiness.chron.com/can-cultural-differences-affect-business-communication-5093.html.

Zeman, Eric. *'Long, Rambling Messages' Most Hated Voicemail Vexation,* Information Week, last modified December 6, 2010, www.informationweek.com/news/smb/mobile/228600099.

Irvine, Christine. *Voice Messaging*, Encyclopedia of Business and Finance, 2nd ed. (2007), accessed January 01, 2012, http://www.encyclopedia.com/doc/1G2-1552100321.html.

Americans Spend More Than One Billion Hours Annually on Voicemail, Business Wire (2012), accessed May 3, 2012, http://www.businesswire.com/news/home/20101206005230/.

Goldman, David. *Facebook Tops 900 Million Users*, CNN Money, accessed May 12, 2012, http://money.cnn.com/2012/04/23/technology/facebook.

Joel Kurtzman Bio, accessed March 3, 2012, http://www.kurtzmangroup.com/joel_kurtzman.php.

Dickinson, Katy, Jankot, Tanya, Gracon, Helen. *Sun Mentoring: 1996–2009*, accessed January 31, 2015, spcoast.com/pub/Katy/SunMentoring1996-2009. smli_tr-2009-185.pdf.

The Internet Movie Database, accessed October 5, 2012, http://www.imbd.com.

CONTRIBUTORS

Teresa Marinelli

Teresa Marinelli is a personal and professional advisor offering both solid, traditional business wisdom and expertise in the metaphysical sciences. Learn about her unique transformational techniques at www.teresamarinelli.com

Suze Yalof Schwartz

Suze is an internationally recognized fashion editor, stylist and TV personality. Her latest venture, Unplug Meditation, is a unique guided meditation studio in Los Angeles, CA. Visit the website: *www.unplugmeditation.com*

Donna Serdula

Donna Serdula is the author of the book, *Professional Secrets to a POWERFUL LinkedIn Profile*, now available on Amazon: *http://amzn.to/LinkedInMakeover*

As a LinkedIn Profile Writer, Donna Serdula has written LinkedIn profiles for executives, entrepreneurs, business owners, government officials, job seekers, and hundreds of other professionals. You can have Donna consult with you on your LinkedIn profile by visiting her website: LinkedIn-Makeover.com

Linda Eve Diamond

Linda Eve Diamond is the author of several books in the areas of business, education, self-help, and poetry. A freelance writer and public speaker living in South Florida, her background includes fifteen years in the corporate training field and three years on the Executive Board of the International Listening Association. In addition to writing, Diamond gives talks and seminars based on her book about listening, *Rule #1: Stop Talking!*, and poetry readings where she shares her most recent poems, along with several from her book, *The Human Experience*. Her websites are *www.LindaEveDiamond.com* and *www.ListenersUnite.com*.

Christine Comaford

New York Times bestselling author Christine Comaford is CEO of Mighty Ventures, an innovation accelerator which helps businesses to massively increase sales, product offerings, and company value. Her triumphs and disasters are revealed in her *New York Times* (and ***USA Today, Wall Street Journal, BusinessWeek,*** and Amazon.com) bestselling business book: *Rules for Renegades: How to Make More Money, Rock Your Career, and Revel in Your Individuality*. The book is available at all major retailers or via *www.RulesForRenegades.com*.

Mark Bowden

Mark Bowden is a world renowned body language expert and creator of TruthPlane, (© Mark Bowden | TruthPlane Inc | 2010)

a communication and presentation training tool used by Fortune 500 companies, CEOs and G7 leaders. For more information, go to *www.truthplane.com*.

David Deasy

An award-winning graphic designer who specializes in business concepts that connect with, excite and motivate people. Check out his impressive portfolio at: *www.behance.net/ddeasy*

Katharine (Kathy) Hansen, Ph.D

Dr. Kathy Hansen, creative director and associate publisher of *Quintessential Careers*, is an educator, author, and blogger. Kathy authored several books, including *Tell Me About Yourself: Storytelling that Propels Careers, Quintessential Careers Press,* ISBN-10: 1-934689-00-9. (April 2009). Visit her web site at *www.astoriedcareer.com*.

Marci Wolf Ober, LMFT

Marci is a licensed family therapist who runs a private practice in Northern New Jersey. She works with adults, adolescents and families to help them live optimally. In addition to speaking frequently on topics such as "Understanding Anxiety" and "Family Dynamics," she lives her beliefs in a wellness lifestyle, and works with destination spas to help their guests take their spa experience home and integrate it into daily living. She can be reached at 973-228-4664.

Rethink Creative Agency

This independent creative agency is one of the most recognized and awarded agencies in Canada. They have offices in Vancouver and Toronto, as well as representation in Montreal. Reach out to Rethink at: *rethinkcanada.com*

Steve Goldner

AKA "SocialSteve," Steve has broad and deep experience as a Marketing Executive. He has served in leadership positions in Social Media, Brand Marketing, Product Marketing, Marketing Communications and Product Management. Steve is Chief Engagement Officer at Social Steve Consulting. Reach Steve on Twitter @SocialSteve or read his blog at *socialsteve.wordpress.com/*

RESOURCES

VISIT THESE SITES for free and insightful personality tests.

Jung Typology Test™
http://www.humanmetrics.com/cgi-win/jtypes2.asp

Disc Personality Test
http://discpersonalitytesting.com/free-disc-test/

CPSIA information can be obtained at www.ICGtesting.com
Printed in the USA
BVOW04s2150150816

459129BV00001B/45/P

9 780988 383401